What a Country!

What a Country!

Dry Bones Looks at Israel

by Ya'akov Kirschen

With an Introduction by Yossi Klein Halevi

THE JEWISH PUBLICATION SOCIETY
Philadelphia • Jerusalem

DRY BONES is syndicated internationally by Cartoonists & Writers Syndicate.

Library of Congress Cataloging-in-Publication Data

Kirschen, Ya'akov.
   [Dry bones (Comic strip).   Selections]
   What a country! : Dry bones looks at Israel / Ya'akov Kirschen ;
with an introduction by Yossi Klein Halevi.
     p.   cm.
   ISBN 0-8276-0572-2 (alk. paper)
   1. Israel—History—Comic books, strips, etc. 2. Caricatures and cartoons—Israel. 3. Israeli wit and humor, Pictorial. I. Title.
DS126.5.K5452   1996
956.94'00207—dc20
                                                     96-942

This book is dedicated to the generations of people who believed in the prophecy of the rebirth of Israel but who did not have the good fortune to live in the time of its fulfillment.

Contents

Preface

When I was ten years old both my baby brother and the State of Israel were born.

In those days, in a Jewish family struggling in an economically challenged section of Brooklyn, we knew that too much praise is "unhealthy." Love meant wanting the members of your family to be as perfect as only they could be, to rise to heights that only we believed they could. Family love was therefore expressed through a constant flow of criticism: "Sit up straight! You'll give yourself a hunchback!" And sarcasm: "You got 98% on a math test? That's wonderful! So what happened to the other two points?" Praise was reserved for occasions when somebody was sick and pride was something expressed to outsiders, as in "He's so brilliant, he got 98% in a math test! What do you think of that?"

Twenty-three years later I moved to Israel, where I now live and work. Here, in the Middle East, I discovered a country that was more like a family than a geopolitical entity. And here, for the past twenty-something years I have been expressing my love for this family/country of mine through an editorial comic strip called *Dry Bones*.

The sarcasm and criticism expressed in these cartoons are the way we Israelis speak about ourselves, and to ourselves, here at home, in the family. The barbs of these cartoons are as sharp as only a deep Jewish love could produce. They have been successful because their local readers understand the language of love and the aspirations for perfection communicated in the "That's wonderful, but what happened to the other two points?" approach to life.

This history of Israel traces my understanding/interpretation of what it has been like living at home ever since I left America, the land of my birth, to "return" to our ancient Semitic homeland. Every cartoon is presented exactly as it appeared when it was first published. I hope that together, as a collection, the cartoons will enable the reader to experience some of the intensity, the pride, and the passion of my live-in love affair with the State of Israel.

YA'AKOV KIRSCHEN
http://drybones.org.il

Acknowledgments

This book would not exist were it not for Toby and Shirley Holtzman. Showing the history of the State of Israel through a collection of *Dry Bones* cartoons was their idea. It was their continued encouragement and assistance that made it possible, and it was Toby's nagging that finally made me decide to roll up my sleeves and do it.

This book might have come into existence as a complete mess without the tireless and creative efforts of Sally Ariel, who began by organizing and photocopying thousands of *Dry Bones* cartoons, and who then went on to select, sort, retouch, edit, and cajole the book into reality.

Kirschen's Israel:
What a Funny Country

by Yossi Klein Halevi

The first Kirschen cartoon that I saw appeared in an obscure, short-lived New York newspaper called the *Jewish Liberation Journal,* whose curious obsession was reconciling Zionism with New Left Marxism. The year was 1970. The cartoon satirized those young Jewish radicals who supported every people's cause but their own, and took the form of a dialogue between a black militant and a fawning Jew:

"My name used to be Jones but that was a slave name," says the black man. "It wasn't African! It was the name of the white Europeans who enslaved my people!"

"Right on," says the Jew.

"English is not the language of my people. I am now studying Swahili!"

"Right on!" exults his supporter. "Could I make a donation to your cause?"

And then the elaborate punchline begins.

"Say," inquires the black man, "isn't your name Steinberg? That's a German name! The name of the white Europeans who murdered one third of your people!"

The Jew smiles condescendingly: "You're not really going to rap about the six million?"

"English is not the language of your people! Are you studying Hebrew?"

The Jew, smiling nervously now, says, "Did you hear the one about the little old Jew who was on a train in Texas . . ."

"Your brothers in the Soviet Union are being cruelly oppressed! Have you ever demonstrated in support of them?"

"Well . . . with my activities on behalf of the Vietnamese, blacks, Indians, there isn't much time."

"Pig!"

The Jew retreats into what appears to be thoughtful silence. But then he suppresses his doubts and, gleefully asserting ideology over reason, asks the black militant with a grin, "Can I still make a donation to your cause?"

Improbably but entirely logically, Kirschen transforms the black revolutionary, whom the reader instinctively assumes to be anti-Zionist, into a spokesman for Jewish pride. In so doing, he disarms our ideological defenses—emulating, as he puts it, the Israeli Air Force's tactic of outwitting enemy radar by flying beneath it. The cartoon is politically unclassifiable: "left-wing" in its identification with the black power agenda, "right-wing" in its insistence on Jewish self-interest. The fact that dozens of Jewish student newspapers, ranging from far left to Kahanist, reprinted the cartoon in the early '70s, proved Kirschen's virtually unique ability among Jewish commentators to appeal across the spectrum.

The elements which made that cartoon so memorable—unexpected twists, disdain for political correctness of any sort, brutal honesty softened by humor—are the hallmarks of Kirschen's great lifework, *Dry Bones,* the cartoon strip on which this book is based. Kirschen began *Dry Bones* in 1973, shortly

after leaving his native New York and moving to Israel. The strip was initially published in the daily newspaper, the *Jerusalem Post,* and later moved to the bi-weekly magazine, the *Jerusalem Report,* when that was founded in 1990. In addition, *Dry Bones* is syndicated in more than three dozen American Jewish weeklies, and is on occasion reprinted by general publications like *Time* magazine and the *New York Times.*

The popularity and staying power of *Dry Bones*—still going strong more than two decades after it first appeared—owes much to Kirschen's ability to defy political and religious categories. He is a deeply religious man who isn't sure he believes in God, a Zionist patriot who revels in exposing Israeli absurdities, a moral critic wary of moral critics. In an Israel transfixed with its own divisiveness, where people instinctively classify and dismiss each other with facile ideological labels, he refuses to be a one-dimensional Jew.

Kirschen, a big man with rumpled white hair, is part Yiddish comedian, part '60s hipster. His speech is slow and bemused, as though every sentence were leading to a punchline. He manages to sound at once low-key and exuberant, an ironic singsong concealing delight.

He was born in Brooklyn in 1938. His family of Russian and Romanian immigrants was nonobservant, but instinctively Jewish. "I wasn't some fish swimming by who doesn't know he's a fish. I had a familial attachment to the Jews: They were my street gang."

But his real passion was comic books, which he read late at night by flashlight under the covers. He preferred the "sophisticated" comics—*Captain Marvel,* not *Superman.* And he drew: His first work, at age twelve, was a collection of dinosaur sketches.

The message he got from the grownups around him was that his cartoon obsession was an unfortunate character flaw. Cartooning was not yet seen as an art form, to be taught at universities and published in collected works. And so when he would pick up a comic, his parents would say, "Why don't you read a good book?" And when his father showed a family friend Ya'akov's dinosaur drawings, the reaction was: "Those aren't dinosaurs, they're *cartoons* of dinosaurs."

Kirschen internalized the message and felt vaguely ashamed of his obsession. "Cartooning was something I was expected to outgrow." At Queens College he studied "real" art, intending to become a painter. He did draw cartoons, because he couldn't help himself: He was good, and they made people laugh. He even published several in *Playboy;* but then stopped submitting to the magazine, afraid that cartooning would become a profession, rather than a lark.

After graduation, he began painting. For a living, he worked as a consultant in the nascent computer industry, running seminars for corporate executives on how to use their machines. "I was successful because I wasn't ashamed to speak on the most basic possible level. I would begin by saying, 'Okay, now here's the switch. You can tell the computer is on when you hear a humming noise.'" In fact, he was implementing his cartoonist's ability to simplify complex issues.

In the mid-1960s, Kirschen became an anti-Vietnam War activist. He would draw cartoons opposing the conflict, run them off on a mimeo machine and distribute them on street corners. "You were supposed to write tomes against the war, not cartoons. But I found that cartoons could get people to say 'Aha,' in a way that the tomes sometimes couldn't. It wasn't fair, it wasn't supposed to

happen that way, but it worked." He was still far from accepting himself as a cartoonist, but for the first time he felt a certain respect for his work: Cartoons could not only make people laugh but make them *understand*.

In 1968, Kirschen was elected a Manhattan delegate to the Democratic Party Convention in Chicago, representing anti-war candidate Eugene McCarthy. Because of his new status, he began receiving mail from political groups across the country. "Every imaginable organization sent me stuff. It got to the point where my mailman would literally bring me sacks of mail. But I noticed that no Jewish organizations sent me their material. I found that curious."

When he got to the Chicago Democratic Convention, his curiosity turned to confusion: Hundreds of groups had sent lobbyists—but no Jewish group was among them. "I'd always assumed the Jews were taken care of. After all, they had so many organizations. But now I began to wonder: If they're so fixed up, why aren't they pushing their causes?"

When the convention ended, he looked up the word "Zionist" in the Manhattan phone book. "I found something called the Zionist Organization of America and arranged a meeting with its president, the chief Zionist." Kirschen asked the man why no Zionist organization had contacted him or the other delegates to the Democratic National Convention. The chief Zionist said, "We don't need people like you. We talk to the people at the top. We talk to the president." And he abruptly ended the meeting. Kirschen began to suspect that the Jews needed all the help they could get.

"I made the rounds in the Jewish community and discovered that the people who had their heads together weren't part of the big organizations but were marginalized. I joined the Student Struggle for Soviet Jewry, a handful of misfits who were saving Soviet Jewry *despite* the establishment. I got involved with crazies like the Radical Zionist Alliance where they debated whether they were Jewish socialists or socialist Jews." And he drew cartoons for "alternative" papers like the *Jewish Liberation Journal*.

Kirschen's growing Jewish commitment was stimulated by the black power movement. "Blacks were demanding to know their own history and I thought, Great! But what about me? Why had I been taught that 1492 was when Columbus discovered America, but not taught that that was when the Jews were expelled from Spain? Why was I accepting the white man's history as my own?" In a sense, Kirschen himself was that young Jewish leftist in his cartoon, listening to the black revolutionary lecture him about his identity, except that in Kirschen's case, the cartoon ended with the Jew accepting the black man's argument and rejoining his people.

At the time, Kirschen was making periodic trips to Harlem. He had joined the National Guard; and the closest National Guard unit to his home was in Harlem. Though only one of three whites among a thousand blacks, he felt at home there. He had always been drawn to black culture: Growing up in the black-Jewish neighborhood of Fort Green, he would eavesdrop on the gospel music coming from the churches.

It was in the Harlem National Guard that Kirschen began seeing himself as a Jewish humorist. "One day, we're sitting through one of those interminable lectures by some uptight officer, when he calls on a friend of mine: 'You've got a light plane on a dark airstrip; what's the first thing you do to camouflage it?' My friend struggles to his feet like some *Amos 'n' Andy* character and starts to answer in a slow-witted drawl. There are four possible answers, and he picks something obviously wrong. Now I know my friend isn't dumb: He's a college student. But he's making himself sound dumb. The officer starts talking down to him, and finally says in exasperation: 'It's a light-colored plane, okay?' 'Oh,' my friend says, 'light-*colored*. I thought you meant light*weight*. Because if it was lightweight, then my answer would have been right, now wouldn't it?'

"Suddenly I realize: Blacks mock authority by playing dumb, so that the white man never knows when he's being put on. And I realize something else: *My* culture's humor works in the opposite way, by proving to authority how smart you are, how you're not being taken in. During lectures I would make some wiseass remark and crack up everyone in the room, and I'd be penalized. But my black friends never got caught, they never had to sweep up the classroom and miss the smoking break, because even when everyone laughed at their routines, the lecturer couldn't pin it on them! They'd learned to shuffle, I'd learned to tell jokes. Different survival strategies. It meant that I wasn't just an independent individual, but was acting out my people's culture without even knowing it."

Meanwhile, Kirschen continued painting. He wanted to contribute to the Jewish people as an artist; and so he decided to write a book on the history and philosophy of Jewish art. The book never got written; but it nevertheless changed his life.

One day, while researching Jewish symbols in the Bible, he began reading the Book of Ezekiel. He came to Chapter 37, the vision of the resurrecting dry bones: "Son of man, these bones are the whole house of Israel. Behold, they say, 'Our bones are dried up, and our hope is lost. . . .' O my people, I will open

your graves . . . and you shall live, and I will place you in your own land."

Kirschen was stunned. He recalled the photographs he had seen of the death camps, the bones piled like kindling, and he thought: This guy *knew*. Somehow, Ezekiel had written a letter 2,600 years ago and addressed it to Ya'akov Kirschen, to the generation of the Holocaust and Israel's rebirth.

Kirschen didn't believe in God; but he couldn't dismiss Ezekiel. "I believed Ezekiel was true because I could see no other logical option. It's like following a map: There's a wiggle on the map, you go through a wiggle on the road; a hill on the map, you go over a hill. Who wrote that map? Who cares? It's a map, it seems to be working, I'll use it. The denial of Ezekiel requires faith—a belief in the secular principles of the twentieth century."

Kirschen remained a nonpracticing Jew, but he decided to become a practicing Zionist—by moving to Israel. He had never visited there, but that seemed to him irrelevant. He could imagine no greater adventure than participating in the fulfillment of Ezekiel's vision. "Growing up in New York, you don't want to live in the sticks but at the center. Suddenly, for me, the Big Apple was Israel, not New York. In terms of the history of my people and its future, New York was a backwater."

Kirschen and his wife and three daughters arrived in Jerusalem as immigrants in October 1971. He came without expectations, and so he wasn't disappointed. "I didn't care which particular Zionist ideology won, only that Israel should survive and be a moral place. All Zionism meant to me was that you should go home. You go home not because it's wonderful, but because it's yours."

Kirschen insisted on moving to an immigrant absorption center— temporary subsidized housing where immigrants study Hebrew—located in a Jerusalem neighborhood populated by working-class Sephardim (Jews of Middle Eastern origin), rather than

4

to the absorption center in a middle-class suburb which a well-meaning Zionist official had suggested. Kirschen became friendly with the Sephardi kids who played in the street outside the building; he delighted to encounter Israel's variety of Jewish ethnicity, humanity in microcosom which the In-gathering of the Jews had produced. Living in Israel became for him an ongoing education, a rediscovery of the complexity of the Jewish people. "Everything was familiar, but a little bit different. They celebrated Hanukkah, but ate jelly donuts instead of latkes. What a funny country."

He quickly discovered the flaws in Ezekiel's dream landscape. "Israel managed to combine German politeness with Arab efficiency"—that is, integrate every ethnic group's worst traits into its national character. But rather than feel aggrieved, or blame Zionist reality for betraying Zionist ideals, his survival strategy was to appreciate the country's absurdities.

He began posting cartoons on the absorption center's bulletin board, at once reflecting and deflecting with humor the complaints of his fellow immigrants about the way things worked and didn't work in their new country. The cartoons became so popular that he decided to send some to the *Jerusalem Post*. They were accepted; and the first *Dry Bones* appeared on January 1, 1973.

The title of the cartoon strip came, of course, from Ezekiel: "All I was doing was writing footnotes to Ezekiel. He put it all down, he just didn't know the clerks would be so rude."

Dry Bones became Israel's first political cartoon strip—and the first anywhere, notes Kirschen, to use the traditional cartoon devices of boxed scenes and balloons for dialogue. With *Dry Bones,* Kirschen finally acknowledged that he was a professional cartoonist. He compares the process of his artistic self-acceptance to that of becoming a conscious Jew: Both were conditional on freeing himself from society's judgments.

Unlike other cartoonists, who thought they would dignify their works by calling them "drawings," Kirschen insisted on calling them what they were—cartoons. To disguise cartooning with euphemism, he thought, was like American Jews trying to assimilate and become white. So fully did Kirschen identify with his cartoon strip that friends began calling him "Bones."

Kirschen's alter ego, and the star among the *Dry Bones* cast of characters, is Shuldig, the middle-aged former American whose ironic but generous sensibility provides a running commentary on Israeli life. Shuldig exudes a weary but enduring idealism, a deep pessimism about Israel's short-term fate, and an almost messianic optimism about its long-term prospects.

The name "Shuldig" means "guilty" in Yiddish; and Kirschen initially created him as a fall guy: When something went wrong in the country, Shuldig was supposed to take the blame. "It seemed strange to me that in the Diaspora, Jews always felt guilty about everything, but that when we finally returned home, no one felt guilty about anything."

Kirschen intended Shuldig as the antidote to a man named M. Schiffman, the spokesman for the Egged bus cooperative. "Whenever someone would write a letter to the *Jerusalem Post* complaining about a rude bus driver—'A driver slammed the door on my foot and dragged me three blocks'— M. Schiffman would write that Egged's drivers were always the first to respond to the country's crises and how dare anyone criticize these wonderful patriots. So I thought, What this country needs is that unique character who would take responsibility. Just say, 'I admit it, I'm guilty and I'm sorry. *Ich bin shuldig.*'"

But a funny thing happened to Shuldig on the way to the drawing board: Kirschen couldn't get him to take the blame. Instead, Shuldig became the Israeli Everyman, a kind of ombudsman of the country's emotions and frustrations, the little citizen angry about corrupt politicians and bureaucrats who are the very opposite of "civil servants"—not to mention Yasser Arafat masquerading as a man of peace, *Newsweek*'s refusal to include Jerusalem in its map of Israel, and American pressure on its democratic Israeli ally to surrender strategic territory to Arab dictators. "Shuldig is the sort of Jewish uncle who isn't religious or anti-religious, the Jack Benny in the family, not antagonistic, but when he gets angry you know it must be really bad."

Shuldig is almost subversively suspicious of authority. Israel as seen through *Dry Bones* is generally governed by slapstick incompetence and even vague malevolence. Kirschen sometimes uses King Solomon to symbolize Israel's leadership, and it is not a flattering portrayal. The king is self-centered, autocratic, and actually enjoys adding to the burdens of his over-taxed, bureaucracy-bound people. In one cartoon, Solomon and his advisers try to one-up each other on devising outrageous new decrees. They consider imposing a hefty travel tax to leave the country—a tax which in fact once existed and is one of *Dry Bones*'s favorite examples of government absurdity. Then, as Solomon and his aides muse on, their ideas become increasingly surrealistic. "Pebbles!" enthuses an aide. "We make them walk with pebbles in their shoes!" "Can't enforce it," says Solomon. "Okay," agrees the aide, "so how 'bout we make them wear hooks in their noses?" Solomon smiles. "I'll write it down," says the aide.

Kirschen's suspicion of leaders has several sources. First, there is the cartoonist's '60s background, with its instinctive aversion to power. In Bob Dylan's words: "Don't follow leaders/watch the parkin' meters." That disdain is reinforced by Kirschen's Holocaust consciousness: Like many of his generation, he sees the near-total failure to rescue European Jewry as a failure of Jewish leadership.

Finally, there is Kirschen's Israeli experience. His formative moment as an Israeli came two years after his arrival in the country—during the 1973 war, when a combined Egyptian and Syrian assault on Yom Kippur caught the Jewish state almost totally unprepared. After the unimagined victory of the 1967 Six-Day War, Israelis had come to blindly trust the reassurances of their military and political leaders, who insisted that the country was never more secure and that the Arabs wouldn't dare attack for decades. There was even a Hebrew word for the leadership's arrogant self-confidence: *smokh*—Trust me. And so, when the country was nearly overrun in October 1973, the sense of betrayal among Israelis was profound, and ever since, they have compensated for their earlier trust with an almost dogmatic wariness toward their leaders.

Kirschen's suspicion of authority is the soul of Jewish humor—the wiseguy mocking power. According to Kirschen, the first recorded Jewish joke was a biblical jab at Moses' leadership. As the Jews are standing before the Red Sea, with the as-yet-unparted waters before them and Egypt's chariots closing in from behind, they call out to Moses: There weren't any graves in Egypt? Is that why you've brought us here to die?

"In their moment of crisis," asks Kirschen, "what do the Jews do? They turn on their great leader and make a cynical joke! 'You think you fooled us, Moses? We went along with the program, but we knew it would turn out badly from the beginning.' You can imagine the people who wrote the Bible, sitting around and saying, 'Hey what about that line about the graves in Egypt? That's too good to leave out.' And you can almost hear some Israeli soldier saying to Labor Party leaders in the next war, 'That's why you gave up the Golan Heights to the Syrians: so I wouldn't have to drive so far to get to the front!'"

Kirschen's choice of Solomon as symbol of Israel's scheming and duplicitous politicians underscores the Jewish comic's irreverence toward authority. In Jewish lore, Solomon is depicted as a wise arbiter, the spiritual giant who built the Jerusalem Temple. Less emphasized, though, are Solomon's excesses: He took a thousand wives, taxed his people beyond endurance, and left behind an incompetent heir who presided over the division of the kingdom into rival Israelite and Judean states. It is that legacy which Kirschen draws on in his ruthlessly unsentimental portrait of Solomon; and the comic's message to the king is: Maybe you can fool the other Jews, but you can't fool *me*.

Kirschen's assumption that our leaders aren't any smarter—and are often considerably dumber—than the rest of us has been periodically confirmed by reactions of the powers-that-be to some of *Dry Bones*'s more preposterous ideas. During tense negotiations in the mid-1970s between Israel and Egypt over partial withdrawal from the Sinai desert, for example, Kirschen offered a "proposal" which he assumed was a self-evident parody: Drill holes into Sinai and sink it. By turning Sinai into a sea, he continued, no one could claim sovereignty over it and, as an added bonus, the desert city of Beersheva would become a deep-sea port.

Shortly after the cartoon appeared, Kirschen got a call from the officer in charge of the map room at the United Nations: The man wanted the original of the "sink the Sinai" cartoon, for inclusion in the UN archive of Sinai peace plans. "You mean you think it's a good plan?" Kirschen asked incredulously. "It's makes more sense than many and as much sense as some," replied

the official. Kirschen gave him the original drawing, which presumably remains on file in the UN's map room.

Says Kirschen, "When you go to a carpenter, he's supposed to know more about carpentering than you. A politician or a government official is supposed to understand more about how the world works than we do. But then I do some *Dry Bones* peace plan and I find out that the people in charge think my crazy ideas are as good as anything they've come up with. It's pretty frightening."

Like Israel itself, this book staggers between war and peace—or more precisely, between war and lower levels of hostility. There is no linear progression here, no anticipated happy ending in a grand new Middle East. Instead, cynicism and hope intermingle: Terrorist attacks accompany peace talks, while civilian normalcy persists during war.

The Israel of *Dry Bones* is a rejected lover, pursuing the vision of peace like a fantasist longing for the ideal woman. Egypt's President Sadat lands almost dream-like at Ben Gurion Airport, and Israel rewards the overture by withdrawing from all of Sinai; but then Sadat is assassinated, and his successor, Hosni Mubarak, stymies all but the most formal relations with the Jewish state. Yasser Arafat and Yitzhak Rabin shake hands on the White House lawn, but the PLO leader continues to incite the Palestinians to holy war. Despite rumors of peace, the reality is increasing violence. *Dry Bones* echoes the sarcastic despair of the Prophet Jeremiah: "Peace, peace, but there is no peace."

Kirschen is prepared to compromise for peace—real peace. But that doesn't seem to be what the Arabs are offering. Instead, he smells a setup: Unable to defeat Israel on the battlefield, the Arabs are trying to weaken it

through "land for peace"—a "piece of paper" peace which they intend to abrogate once Israel has paid in the hard currency of strategic territory. Kirschen's advice to his people is the venerable message of the Jewish comic: Don't be taken for a fool.

But because the Jewish comic examines every ideological platform for the fine print, Kirschen's ambivalence extends not only to the Israeli left but also the right. He understands its motives and shares its anger at a world in which Jews, even after Auschwitz, can't find peace. But he won't endorse any ideology which promises instant salvation— whether "peace now" or "security now." He demands of the right precisely what he demands of the left: to accommodate ideology to reality, not the other way around.

Kirschen is especially wary of those religious Jews who justify the unjustifiable, like the Purim 1994 massacre of Muslim worshippers in Hebron's Tomb of the Patriarchs. Kirschen is on to the fatal contradiction of Israel's religious right: insisting on Jewish chosenness, even while acting like everyone else—the mirror image of anti-Zionists, who demonize Israel for behaving no better than any other country.

The nearly three-decades-long debate over the status of Judea and Samaria, or the West Bank, runs through this book—and through Kirschen. One can almost hear him haranguing himself: Return to eight-mile-wide borders in one of the world's most unstable regions—what are you, crazy? Remain in the territories and become a permanent conqueror—for this we created a Jewish state?

Those looking for a clear political line in *Dry Bones* will be disappointed. There are "right-wing" West Bank cartoons, like the one about a TV journalist announcing into a camera that the rioters being filmed are "calling for simple justice"; but then, discovering that they aren't Palestinians but Jewish settlers, he does a second take which begins, "Today's story is one of extremism and hate." And there are "left-wing" West Bank cartoons: Israeli soldiers "accidentally" beat some American journalists, explaining, "We thought they were civilians." The only consistency here is *Dry Bones*'s insistence on telling the truth.

The future of the territories is Israel's great self-confrontation—not least because it forces Jews to make sense of their past. The Holocaust imposes on Jews two nonnegotiable demands: Don't treat the stranger as you were treated; and never minimize your enemy's intentions. But the Israeli left and right have each appropriated one of those imperatives, ignoring the other. The left is guilty of a remarkable naiveté toward the malevolent reality of the Middle East, while the right too easily accepts the ground rules of that reality, entering its brutality without squeamishness.

After the Holocaust, insists Kirschen, Jews are forbidden to be brutal, forbidden to be naive. Fittingly, his rejection of the occupation seems to grow in direct proportion to his skepticism of the Arabs' commitment to peace. He is cursed with the comic's vision: He can't ignore reality.

Ask Kirschen what Israel should do and he'll tell you, "Don't ask me, I'm just the cartoonist." His job is to expose our delusions. And so *Dry Bones* offers critiques, not proposals. But that is precisely its gift to the Jewish people: to embody complexity, to embrace the impossible paradoxes of our dilemma without opting for easy answers, caricatures of political solutions.

If Israel's political and religious debates are often so intolerant, so hysterical, that is because its protagonists believe that if their opponents prevail, the country will not just decline, but self-destruct. For right-wingers, an Israel reduced to crippled borders will be-

come an irresistible target for a pan-Arab invasion, which the Jewish state might not survive. Left-wingers are equally convinced that annexing the West Bank will erode Israeli democracy and our faith in the justice of our cause, end whatever foreign support we enjoy, and leave us totally isolated—ultimately destroying us.

The apocalyptic nature of the territorial debate extends, though more subtly, to the secular-religious divide. Orthodox Jews fear that turning Eretz Yisrael into a Westernized, hedonistic society will once again provoke God's anger: Twice we were expelled from the Holy Land for violating its sanctity; and our miraculous return home is conditional on our finally learning to respect its uniqueness. Secular Jews are equally insistent that Israel can survive in the Middle East only by maintaining the edge that modern, democratic societies enjoy over totalitarian ones; that if the Jewish state becomes a medieval theocracy, it is doomed.

Kirschen empathizes with all those fears. For him, almost every Jewish ideology is legitimate, or at least contains some essential truth learned by Jews through historical experience. His vision of the Jewish people is holistic: Each group is a vital organ, contributing to the well-being of the body. Like the great Yiddish humorists, Kirschen loves his Jews, even when they disappoint and infuriate him—which happens often, because he also knows his Jews. He exposes their failures with a sigh, not an accusing finger. He is never vicious or hateful; and that is what makes him an artist, rather than a mere caricaturist.

If most Jewish ideologies are at least partially true, each also contains a common, fatal flaw—the certainty that it alone knows the meaning and purpose of Jewish history, that its way is the only way for a Jew to act and believe. Kirschen can't bear the tendency of Jews to not merely argue with each other, but to actually demonize one another. He understands them all, because there is a little bit of each of them in him; and they all confound him, because they refuse to understand each other.

He expects more from his people—from the generation of the resurrected dry bones—than mutual delegitimization. The growing hatred among Jews, he believes, is far more dangerous to their survival than the triumph of any one of their competing ideologies.

West Bank settlers and peace activists, religious fanatics and secular fanatics—no one is immune from Kirschen's disdain for hypocrisy and self-aggrandizement. Ideologues of every persuasion are forewarned: Before claiming Kirschen as "one of us," keep turning the pages of this book; sooner or later you'll probably find yourself on the wrong end of a *Dry Bones* joke.

For all their passion, *Dry Bones*'s Israelis are normal people trying to live uneventful lives in the midst of too much history. Here is Shuldig, musing: "Amazing how history repeats itself. Once again a U.S. envoy shuttles back and forth . . . Once again the condemnation of the world is directed at us . . . And once again it's too late to start a diet to get into shape for a bathing suit."

The border between the individual and the collective is constantly being violated. *Dry Bones* captures that remarkable Israeli agility which almost unconciously shifts from the personal to the political and back again: No matter what the conversation, one can usually ask an Israeli about "the situation" without seeming intrusive, because, somewhere in his head, the country's fate is being considered.

Though they try, Israelis cannot evade "the situation." Consider Shuldig, muttering about "West Bank, the Russians, inflation . . ." as he heads toward the beach, sun umbrella

in hand, for an afternoon of escape; and then, at the end of the day, carrying his umbrella home and muttering about the very same concerns. And when Shuldig returns from abroad, a friend congratulates him, because he's already been back for two days and hasn't once listened to the news.

Dry Bones's Israel suffers from an excess of life. It is a country crowded with too many survivors from too many traumas pressing against each other in too little space; a country where every family member has an army-issued gas mask stored in the closet, but whose religious people are messianists and whose secular people mere optimists; an almost unbearable convergence point of conflicting visions and insoluble moral dilemmas, where ideologues shout on street corners over the identical issues they've been debating for decades; where trips abroad aren't considered vacations but escapes and whose happiest place is Ben Gurion Airport, which Israelis leave and return to with equal relief; a chameleon-like country whose borders change with each new war and whose society changes with every immigration; where nothing can be taken for granted, least of all existence, and whose people therefore know to appreciate simple pleasures; a country where corruption and idealism coexist in seemingly equal measure, where people cheat each other and die for each other; an irreverent, religion-obsessed society where nothing is sacred and everything is sacred, which dares to turn a holy land into kitsch and transform biblical myth into reality; a place to which so many extravagant dreams have been trusted and whose reality often seems so mediocre; where dreams are constantly violated and new dreams just as quickly take their place.

Though this book covers little more than two decades, it manages to include three wars (the Yom Kippur War of 1973, the Lebanon War of 1982, and the Gulf War of 1991), a Palestinian uprising, hyper-inflation and economic boom, mass immigration, the rise of the right to power in 1977, the return of the left in 1992, and the Right's surprise victory in 1996. Several distinct Israels emerge here. Indeed, the country is constantly reinventing itself—so abruptly and profoundly that it seems unsure of its most basic identity.

The book opens in the months just before the Yom Kippur War. The last vestiges of the Israel of the '50s and '60s—socialist and pioneering—are still tangible. Though slowly becoming westernized, Israel remains provincial; its people view the world beyond their borders as a kind of undifferentiated territory—*hutz la'aretz,* outside the Land of Israel.

Still, the state is moving, in its twenty-fifth year, toward premature mid-life angst. It uneasily occupies the territories it won in the 1967 war, unsure whether to settle them or withdraw, and bearing them like an overweight man whose belly at once marks his prosperity and his youthful decline. Israel is the Middle East superpower, though PLO terror attacks are a constant reality; both war and peace seem far away.

Then comes Yom Kippur, 1973. The country rallies, revealing an instant civility it stores like a secret weapon for times of crisis. Strangers discover camaraderie, old ladies stop pushing on bus lines, the radio broadcasts personal messages to wives and girlfriends from reservists at the front. Shuldig, too, does his part: He squeezes into his tight-fitting "civil guard" uniform and patrols the home front. Like Israeli society, he looks civilian even in uniform.

Israel glimpses its mortality during the surprise Yom Kippur attack; and the aftermath of war is almost equally traumatic. The Arab oil boycott turns most of the world's governments, including those of Western

Europe, against Israel. Kirschen knows Israel isn't always just in its treatment of the Palestinians; but he knows too that, fundamentally, Israel is on the right side of the Middle East conflict. Israel isn't being criticized for specific failures but demonized, turned into a symbol of evil whose right to exist is reexamined after each moral lapse; and that, insists Kirschen, is nothing more than an updated version of classical anti-Semitism. Through Shuldig, he wages his counterattack: Shuldig is wry about Israel's dysfunctional bureaucrats, and the moral failures of his countrymen perplex and sadden him; but when confronting the anti-Israel hostility of foreign governments and media, his reaction is pure rage.

Spunky little Israel, once admired by the West and much of the Third World, becomes a pariah. Far more countries now recognize the PLO—a gang including hijackers and child murderers—than recognize the sovereign Jewish state. Zionism had promised to "normalize" the Jews—transform them from a permanent, despised minority into a nation like all others. But now, Jewish history has come full circle, turning the Jews into a despised nation-state. A Jewish joke: Zionism, the Jews' boldest attempt to escape their fate, has merely created new circumstances for their delegitimization. The state of the Jews, notes Israeli historian J. L. Talmon in a bitter one-liner worthy of Shuldig, has become the Jew of the states.

A "new Israel" emerges, doubtful of its future and its place among the nations. The new Israel finds its face in right-wing Likud leader Menachem Begin, for whom the Jewish state is a fortress refuge in a hostile world. In 1977, Begin is elected prime minister, displacing the Labor Party which has ruled the country since its birth. The immediate pretext for Labor's defeat is corruption in high places; but the country's international isolation and deepening sense of siege grants Begin's hard-line Zionism a new validity.

Israel begins settling the West Bank in earnest, refusing to return to its absurdly vulnerable pre-1967 borders. Foreign observers detect a nation driven by arrogance and messianic delusion. And yet Israel is arguably the first conqueror to worry that withdrawing from territory won't merely diminish but destroy it. Except for a minority of Orthodox ideologues, Israel settles the territories not out of messianic hope but apocalyptic dread.

By the 1980s, Israel is well on its way to becoming an international outlaw. The Israeli invasion of Lebanon in 1982, meant to destroy the PLO's terrorist "state within a state," followed by the Intifada, the Palestinian uprising beginning in late 1987, alienates even many of Israel's friends.

The early pioneering Zionists imagined a Jewish state that would be externally normalized—in harmony with the world—and internally exceptional—a "light to the nations." But Israel of the 1980s seems to have reversed that vision: externally abnormal, morally unexceptional.

And then come the 1990s. As usual, the totally unexpected happens and yet another "new Israel" emerges. The collapse of the Soviet Union, the Gulf War and the ensuing Arab-Israeli peace talks, all combine to break the diplomatic ghettoization of the Jewish state. Almost every day the local papers report on yet another country in Eastern Europe or the Third World seeking ties with Israel. Jerusalem, the solitary city, is suddenly a political and economic pilgrimage site.

But not only is Israel becoming externally normalized; internally, too, it is thriving. While fewer immigrants arrived in Israel during the 1980s than in any other decade in the country's history, the '90s transforms it, once

11

again, into an immigrant society. Hundreds of thousands of Soviet Jews, the most educated immigrants in the country's history, converge on Ben Gurion Airport; and thousands of black Jews are rescued in a last-minute airlift from the Ethiopian war zone, descending from planes barefoot and white-robed, wide-eyed and silent. The Ingathering of the Jews, says Shuldig, is like a broken faucet: Just when you think the pipes have gone dry, water spurts out all over the place.

The immigration stimulates an accelerating prosperity. The Israeli economy records one of the highest growth rates in the world. Shuldig wakes up one morning and discovers an Israel of computers and shopping malls and cable TV and yuppies negotiating over portable phones; even government clerks have become more efficient, if not quite pleasant. One of the key elements of *Dry Bones*'s humor—Israel's cranky inefficiency—is becoming obsolete. Israel of the 1990s *works*.

Inevitably, Kirschen searches for the hidden clause; and the Jewish comic finds it: The new, "normalized" Israel is in danger of losing its soul, of exchanging Jewish culture and intimacy for a superficial westernization. Perhaps the saddest cartoon in this book is the one in which Shuldig, watching cable TV, happily exclaims that Israel is becoming "just like America"—as he slowly metamorphoses into Homer Simpson.

By turning banal, Israel risks betraying the vast sacrifices and expectations which formed it; an unbearable anticlimax to Jewish history. Kirschen is obsessed with the growing amnesia of Israelis: "We're trying hard to forget who we are and why we're here."

In Israel, solving one crisis only creates the conditions for the next one. And so Kirschen

actually misses the musty Israel of rude bus drivers and dictatorial bureaucrats and sales clerks who don't smile and insist you have a nice day but make you pack your own groceries. He realizes that the maddening frustrations of Israeli life have been the price we've paid for a society where people care enough to tell you to your face what they really think of you.

And yet, Kirschen—nonbelieving mystic—suspects that Israel can never become truly "normal." "Israelis can pretend to be Americans all they want, but meanwhile they're the front-line targets of a Muslim holy war to conquer the world, just as Hitler had to first clear away the Jews before establishing the Thousand-Year Reich." He sees the Zionist attempt to normalize Jewish fate in a tiny strip of land holy to three competing religions and located in the midst of the Arab world, as endearing but ludicrous—the ultimate Jewish joke.

The book ends with the murder of Prime Minister Yitzhak Rabin, the pathological expression of Israel's passionate factionalism, and with the assassination's impact on the country's intensified political and cultural divide. But before Israelis can absorb that shock, they are hit with the worst wave of Arab terrorism in the country's history, trauma accumulating upon trauma—and resulting in the return of the Right to power.

Still, however bleak the situation may appear, Kirschen is, like Shuldig, a short-term pessimist and a long-term optimist.

"We've been through impossibly difficult times in this country and more hard times are coming," he says. "But the ship that will carry the Jewish people into the future is Israel. I feel a real sadness for those Diaspora Jews who haven't joined us here, who missed

the boat because they didn't realize what an exhilarating experience it is to come home."

Israel, he believes, will continue to thrive, and perhaps even fulfill the ancient vision of messianic Zion. "Our mission—whether it's been assigned to us by the Creator of the universe or whether it's a self-imposed delusion—is to help heal the planet."

Whatever Israel ultimately becomes, the country is evolving very fast.

One day I phoned Kirschen and read him a letter to the editor from one of the Hebrew dailies, written by the spokesman for the Egged bus cooperative—a successor to M. Schiffman. The letter, headlined, "We Apologize," offered profuse regrets for an incident in which an Arab Israeli passenger, thought to be a terrorist, was mistreated by a bus driver.

"So, Ya'akov," I said, "even Egged is becoming civil."

"They're killing the Zionist dream!" he shouted.

I suspected he was only half-joking.

THE CAST OF CHARACTERS

by Kirschen

Most political cartoons deal with famous faces and events. *Dry Bones* is different. For me, the heroes of this fantastic country and its unbelievable story are the children of Israel who have come home after thousands of years of Diaspora. And so the faces in *Dry Bones* are, for the most part, the faces of the people of Israel, and the "events" that are tracked are the concerns, the dreams, and the fears of the people of this country, which is at once a small family and the home planet of the Jewish galaxy.

In this book you will meet us as we see, and saw, ourselves. The characters most often employed are simple and, to me, real. They are a guy named Shuldig, his dog Doobie, King Solomon and his advisor, two coffee drinkers sitting at a sidewalk café, and two guys discussing the "situation."

Recognizable personalities (from Arafat to Rabin) appear only when they manage to *force* their way into the strip. This happens when they do something that makes commenting on their activities absolutely unavoidable.

Shuldig

Shuldig: Mr. Shuldig is a kindly old-time Zionist, an Israeli Everyman, a member of the family. He is an idealist and an optimist. On some level, Uncle Shuldig is me.

Doobie

Doobie: Doobie the dog lives with Mr. Shuldig. Doobie is a realist and a cynic. He sees himself as a counterbalance to Shuldig's naiveté. He is more of a partner than a pet. He does not think of Shuldig as his "owner," but rather as his "boss."

King Solomon

King Solomon: King Solomon represents the Israeli government in a much deeper way than any prime minister or ruling political party could. He is the state—as opposed to the people.

King Solomon's Advisor

King Solomon's Advisor: In the ancient Middle East he would be called the vizier. In the old days of local socialism, he'd be a party hack. In the final analysis he, like the rest of the public, is simply a foil for the king.

The Coffee Drinkers

The Coffee Drinkers: Being a Mediterranean country, it's only natural that one of our national pastimes is sitting around in coffee houses. We sip a kind of coffee that is so dark and thick that it's called mud (*botz* in Hebrew). In addition to sipping our *botz,* it is traditional to review the newspapers and offer pithy comments on the events of the day.

Two Guys

Two Guys: These are two more characters representing the long-suffering Israeli public. I sometimes think of the guy with the glasses as being Ashkenazi (a Jew whose family came from Europe) and the guy with the mustache as being Sephardi (a Jew from the Arab world). Sometimes I don't.

THE WAY WE WERE

We thought of ourselves as rude, bumbling, bureaucratic, inefficient, and "small time". We also thought of ourselves as the proud new citizens of the miraculously reborn State of Israel–the impossible biblical prophecy come true. The Six-Day War had proven, at last, that the Arab states surrounding us could not destroy us. We were here, home at last, and here to stay. Peace was right around the corner. Soon "our cousins," as we then referred to the Arabs, would accept us as part of the family. Our enemy had now become the bureaucracy of our institutions and the maddening little details of society and state-building. We expected that a massive immigration of Jews from North America was imminent. Zionism was alive and well. Only our befuddled government clerks and the rudeness of our bus drivers seemed to diminish the reality and brightness of the dream come true. "It was the best of times. . . . It was the worst of times."

Like the biblical infiltrators sent by Joshua to spy out the land, we were a little shocked at what we uncovered . . . for starters, the locals were hell on wheels.

Dry Bones

No promise was too impossible in an election year.

Dry Bones

18

Dry Bones

19

Our version of the National Health System was called *Kupat Holim,* the "Sick Fund." We discovered that the "Sick Fund" was, itself, a little sick. But perhaps, with a fresh approach, we could help heal it.

Maybe it's ALWAYS been this way?!

Dry Bones

The Middle Eastern bazaar is called the *shuk*. Like everything else in the Middle East, the ways of the bazaar are a little bizarre.

Dry Bones

We all worked a six-day week, but . . .

We had freedom of travel, but . . .

The national pastime was digging into our past, but . . .

Dry Bones

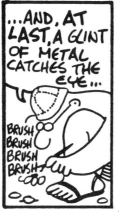

Our hopes and dreams kept us going . . .

Dry Bones

25

Dry Bones

There seemed to be nothing to worry about except where to put up the summer visitors.

Dry Bones

October 1973. We are attacked, it is the Yom Kippur War.

Dry Bones

Dry Bones

Dry Bones

Dry Bones

The attacking Egyptian army has been pushed back, but it seems as if every able-bodied Israeli is needed at the front. Most of our work force having been called into the IDF, our economy begins to stumble. Delivery systems are the first to break down . . . an example is the egg shortage of '73.

Dry Bones

FRIED...

HARD BOILED...

SCRAMBLED..

CHOPPED WITH ONIONS AND MAYONNAISE...

IN A CUP...

THIS HAS BEEN A PUBLIC SERVICE FOR THOSE OF YOU WHO ARE BEGINNING TO FORGET WHAT THEY LOOK LIKE.

© 1973 Kirschen

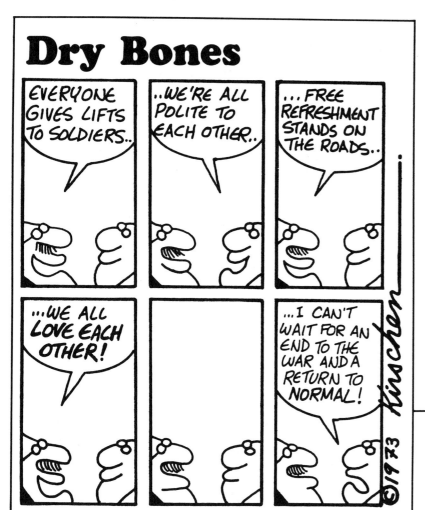

The endless discussion of how and when peace will come to the Promised Land . . .

Another exodus passing over the Red Sea and back to the Holy Land?!

Dry Bones

In Israel a religious party is not a social gathering with kosher food. In Israel a religious party is a political entity that competes for our votes along with our "Democrats" and "Republicans." For example, there's the National Religious Party, the NRP. And, as an example of the kind of issues that it focuses on, there's the question "Who is a Jew?"

Dry Bones

Rumors of an imminent wave of immigration from Russia . . . is our government ready?!

Dry Bones

Money? Who needs it! We've got our love to keep us warm.

Dry Bones

BILLS! BILLS! BILLS!

TENSION! PRESSURE!

I JUST CAN'T GO ON I TELL YOU

I'M GOING TO PUT MY HEAD IN THE OVEN!

HONEY.. THEY JUST TURNED OFF THE GAS

©1974 Kirschen

Dry Bones

I JUST DON'T UNDERSTAND ALL THIS GRUMBLING..

ABOUT THE WEAKNESS OF THE ISRAEL POUND.

LOOK AT THE BRIGHT SIDE!

WE'RE NOT TROUBLED BY COUNTER-FEITERS

THEY WOULDN'T WASTE THEIR TIME!

©1974 Kirschen

We explain nothing!

Dry Bones

SOLOMON, OH WISE KING, YOU HAVE ABOLISHED THE OFFICE OF..

...MINISTER OF INFORMATION...

...COULD YOU GIVE US AN EXPLANATION?

ASK MY MINISTER OF INFORMATION!

BUT THERE **IS** NO MINISTER OF INFORMATION!

©1975 Kirschen

Dry Bones

"WORLD JEWISH CONGRESS PRESIDENT..."

"...NAHUM GOLDMAN SAYS..."

"...HONEYMOON BETWEEN ISRAEL AND THE WORLD HAS ENDED."

HMPHH!

THEY NEVER EVEN **TOLD** ME ABOUT THE **ENGAGEMENT**

©1975 Kirschen

Dry Bones

FITTING IN

The year was 1975. The fantastic hopes of the Six-Day War of 1967 seemed like ancient history. The Yom Kippur War was behind us, and yet, it was still with us. We lived under its shadow. If we had thought in those terms, we would have called it the "Yom Kippur War Syndrome." A sense of "reality" was setting in and we were settling down to see how, in fact, we could "fit in." The country searched for a way to fit in with its neighbors. The new immigrants searched for ways to fit in with the country. We all wondered how to fit in with Diaspora Jews who seemed to be in the process of declining the Zionist invitation to simply pack up and leave the lands of their birth.

We all work a six-day week, but groceries and small shops are closed on Tuesday afternoons, banks and post offices on Wednesday afternoons, and is it on Monday afternoons that barbers and lawyers are closed? An intercity taxi is called a *sherut* and, well, there's just so much to learn before we can fit in.

Dry Bones

Eighteen months after the war and everybody (including Henry Kissinger) seems to have given up on finding a plan for peace . . . or even for a separation of forces. But have no fear . . . Dry Bones is here!

THE DRYBONES PLAN

OK...THE GREATEST MINDS OF THE CENTURY ADMIT DEFEAT, SO IT MUST BE TIME TO UNVEIL ...

THE PROBLEM:

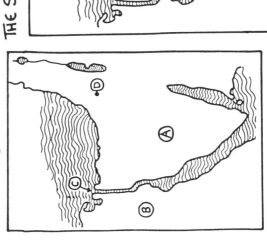

1. ISRAELI AND EGYPTIAN TROOPS FACE EACH OTHER IN AN EXPLOSIVE SITUATION IN SINAI (A)

2. EGYPT (B) BARS ISRAELI SHIPPING FROM THE SUEZ CANAL (C)

3. THERE IS LITTLE, IF ANYTHING, TO DO IN BEERSHEBA (D)

THE SOLUTION:

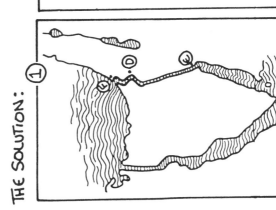

① WE DIG A CANAL FROM EILAT (E) TO GAZA (F) WITH A DETOUR TO BEERSHEBA (D)

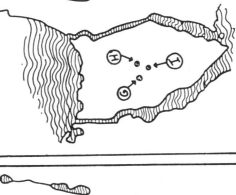

② WE DRILL THREE HOLES (G), (H), +(I)) IN THE MIDDLE OF SINAI

③ SINAI SINKS.

• EGYPT AND ISRAEL ARE SEPARATED BY 200 KM. OF OPEN SEA (J)

• ALL PROBLEMS RELEVANT TO THE SUEZ CANAL HAVE DISAPPEARED.

• BEERSHEBA IS NOW A DEEP WATER PORT (D)

EAT YOUR HEART OUT HENRY, WE THOUGHT OF IT FIRST!

Dry Bones

Dry Bones

Dry Bones

Dry Bonus

We were so poor that . . . !

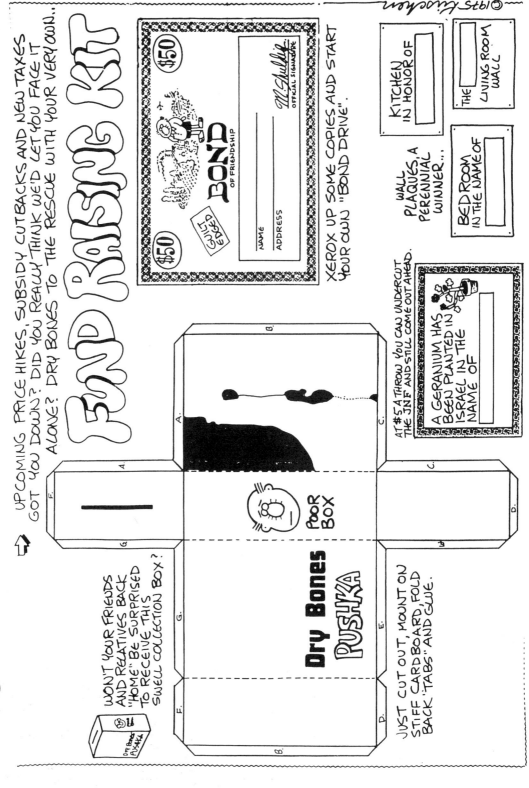

⇪ UPCOMING PRICE HIKES, SUBSIDY CUTBACKS AND NEW TAXES GOT YOU DOWN? DID YOU REALLY THINK WE'D LET YOU FACE IT ALONE? DRY BONES TO THE RESCUE WITH YOUR VERY OWN...

FUND RAISING KIT

$50 $50

BOND OF FRIENDSHIP

GUILT EDGED

NAME _____
ADDRESS _____

M. Shullie
OFFICIAL SIGNATURE

XEROX UP SOME COPIES AND START YOUR OWN "BOND DRIVE".

WALL PLAQUES, A PERENNIAL WINNER...

KITCHEN
IN HONOR OF

THE LIVING ROOM WALL

BED ROOM
IN THE NAME OF

AT #5 A THROW YOU CAN UNDERCUT THE JNF AND STILL COME OUT AHEAD.

A GERANIUM HAS BEEN PLANTED IN ISRAEL IN THE NAME OF

POOR BOX

Dry Bones PUSHKA

JUST CUT OUT, MOUNT ON STIFF CARDBOARD, FOLD BACK "TABS" AND GLUE.

WON'T YOUR FRIENDS AND RELATIVES BACK "HOME" BE SURPRISED TO RECEIVE THIS SWELL COLLECTION BOX?

A. B. C. D. E. F. G.

Dry Bones

Nu? So a *gan* is a nursery school and a *heshbon* is a bill and a *makolet* is a grocery store and a *puncture* is any kind of unexpected difficulty and *vaflim* are a type of cookie and IL200 means 200 Israeli liras (the lira being what we called our Monopoly money before we renamed it the shekel). Giving someone a *tramp* means giving them a lift. And doesn't EVERYBODY know that a *bakbook* is a bottle?! Or have I just "been here too long?"

Dry Bones

We're starting to fit in so well that . . .!

Here in Israel we cross our "sevens" for readability, and we say "it'll be okay" (*Yihyeh tov*) for luck, and (because the floors of our homes are made of twenty centimeter wide stone tiles) it's easy to measure the size of any room you're in (if you're interested in things like room sizes and you understand the metric system).

Dry Bones

Dry Bones

We're starting to fit in so well that we feel free to examine our "alien roots"—the life we lived back in the "Old Country" before aliyah.

The saga continues.

Dry Bones

Dry Bones

THIS PAGE IS SO POOR THAT...

WHAT WITH THE CUT-BACK IN SUBSIDIES AND INCREASES IN PRICES MAYBE IT'S TIME FOR...

POOR SHLDIG'S ALMANAC

"THUNK"?

~RIDDLE~

Q. WHY DO ISRAELI BUTCHERS MAKE FRANKFURTERS HALF BEEF AND HALF SOYA?

SOYA BEEF

A. THEY JUST CAN'T MAKE BOTH ENDS MEAT.

MOTTO TO HANG IN THE KITCHEN...

A QUARTER OF A LOAF IS BETTER THAN NONE.

WE'RE SO POOR THAT WE CAN'T AFFORD AN ALARM CLOCK...

...WE WAKE UP FROM WORRY!

I'M SO POOR THAT MY SHOES HAVE SOLES SO THIN THAT WHEN I STEP ON A BUS TICKET, I CAN TELL YOU THE NUMBER.

WE'RE SO POOR THAT WE'RE SAVING THE BOTTLES 'TIL THE DEPOSITS GO UP.

WE'RE SO POOR THAT AT THIS YEAR'S "SEDER" WHEN WE OPEN THE DOOR FOR ELIJAH WE HOPE HE DOESN'T COME IN.

THEY'RE SO POOR THEY COULD ONLY AFFORD TO GIVE YOU HALF A DRY BONES THIS WEEK

THUNK

WHAT ARE THEY DOING?! TAKING OUR SPACE AWAY?!

SOMETIMES YOU'VE JUST GOT TO...

STAND UP FOR YOUR RIGHTS!!

SOMETIMES THERE ISN'T ENOUGH ROOM TO STAND UP FOR YOUR RIGHTS...

DOBIE the DOG

© 1976 Kirschen

Dry Bones

The Yom Kippur War left us feeling alone and isolated . . . powerless to bring the truth of our position to the media . . . impotent to stop the terrorist attacks against Israelis and Jews around the world. . . . We didn't call it a Yom Kippur War syndrome but it was there, and we all felt it. The planeload of civilians held by terrorists in Uganda's Entebbe Airport seemed to finally crush the country's sinking morale. We silently agreed that we had run out of miracles . . . and then . . .

Dry Bones

The relationship with America has always been a family matter.

Dry Bones

Dry Bones

The Israeli romance with the media seems to have gone a bit sour.

Dry Bones

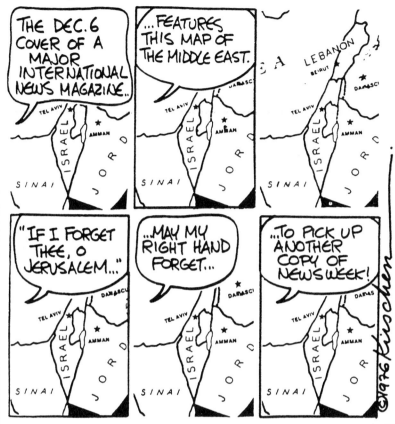

Dry Bones

Dry Bones

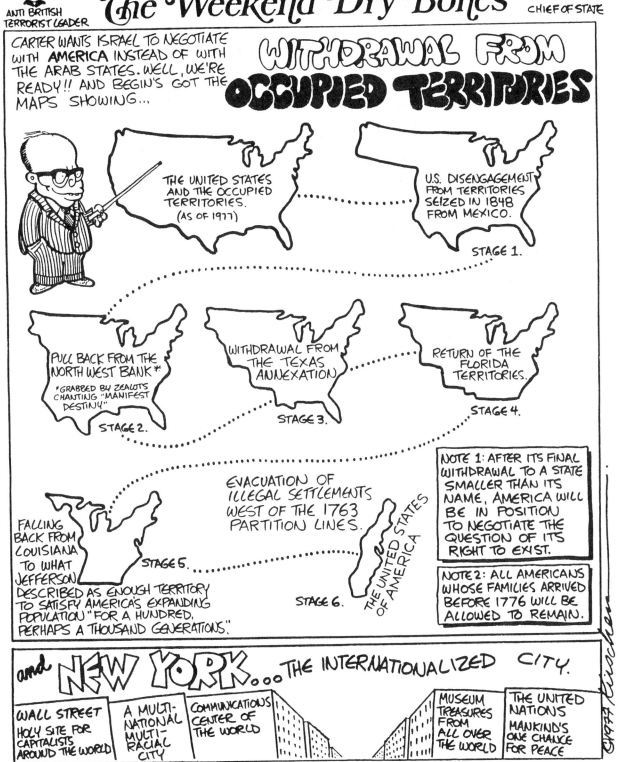

Dry Bones

For generations Moses was the great Law Giver, the great Teacher, the founder of monotheism. But in the *Dry Bones* Israel of 1977, Moses was the one who led us out of Diaspora and back to the Promised Land . . . and so Pessah, or Passover, becomes time to examine the success or failure of the allure of the Zionist dream.

Dry Bones

The traditional Passover meal is called the seder and is, like the American Thanksgiving, a time of great overeating.

Dry Bones

SADAT AND THE SPIRIT OF THE NEW ISRAEL

We didn't know it, but our national mood and Middle East realities were both about to take a major change in direction. What we didn't know was that the president of Egypt was preparing a speech in which he would hold out an olive branch of peace and hope to the Jewish state. What he didn't know was that he would pay for that courageous act with his life. He would be gunned down by Islamic fundamentalists as he reviewed a parade. President Sadat would die a hero to the people of Israel. But all of that was still in our future.

Dry Bones

Look! Up in the sky! . . .

Dry Bones

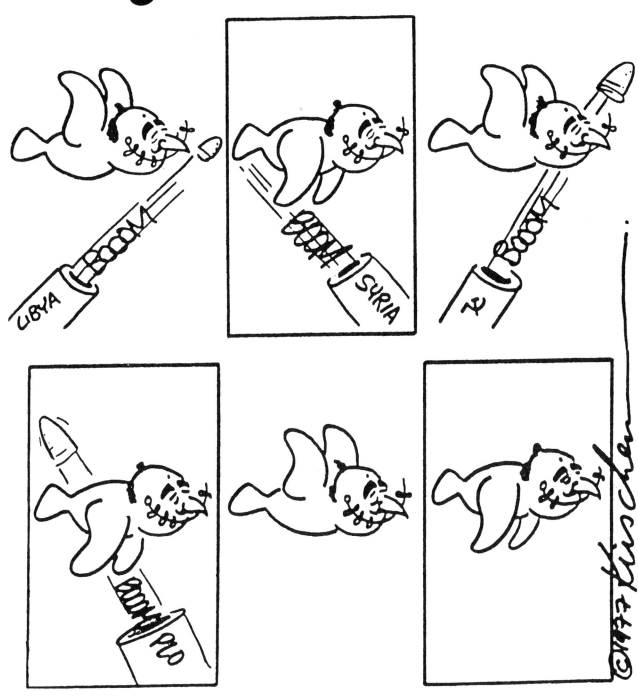

Once again we get that sneaky feeling!

Dry Bones

We get on with the business of trying to deal with our domestic "insanity." The carnage on our highways just won't let up. Could it be related to the attitudes of the Israeli male driver? What others call being macho we call being a *gever*.

Sadat flies to Israel . . . we line the roads and cheer! He addresses the Knesset . . . and then, suddenly . . . it's all over?!

Dry Bones

A moment in history in a wink.

Then, as ever. Assad, the Syrian dictator, keeps an eye on Hussein, the Jordanian king (thought to be "soft" on Israel).

Dry Bones

The Weekend Dry Bones

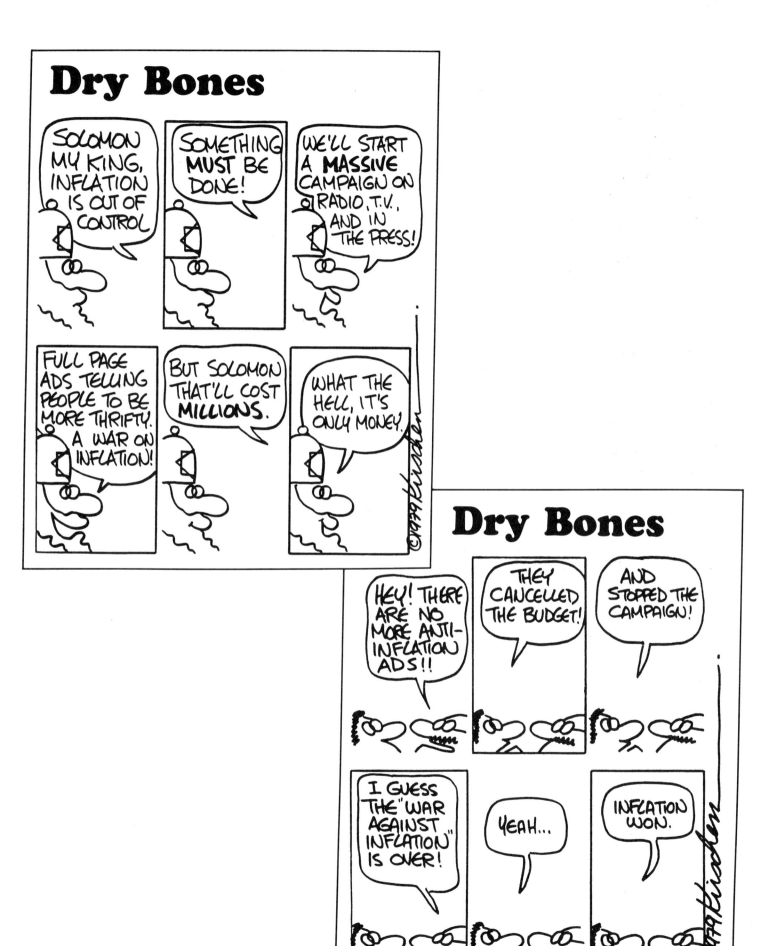

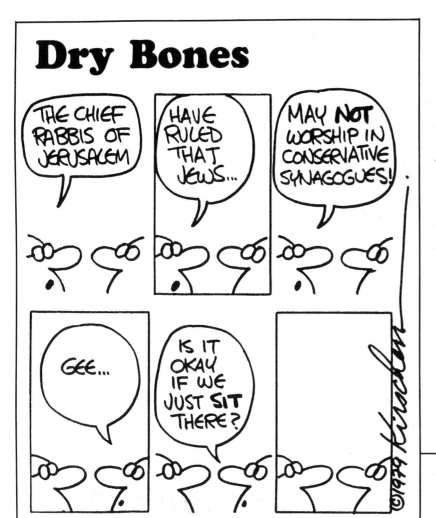

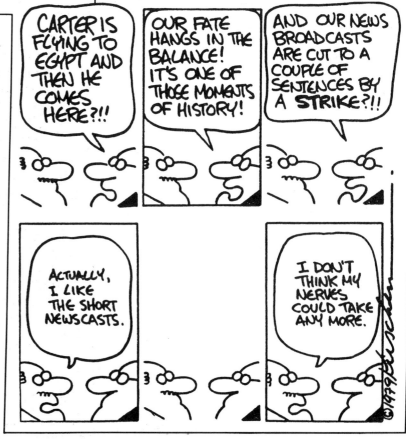

The Weekend Dry Bones

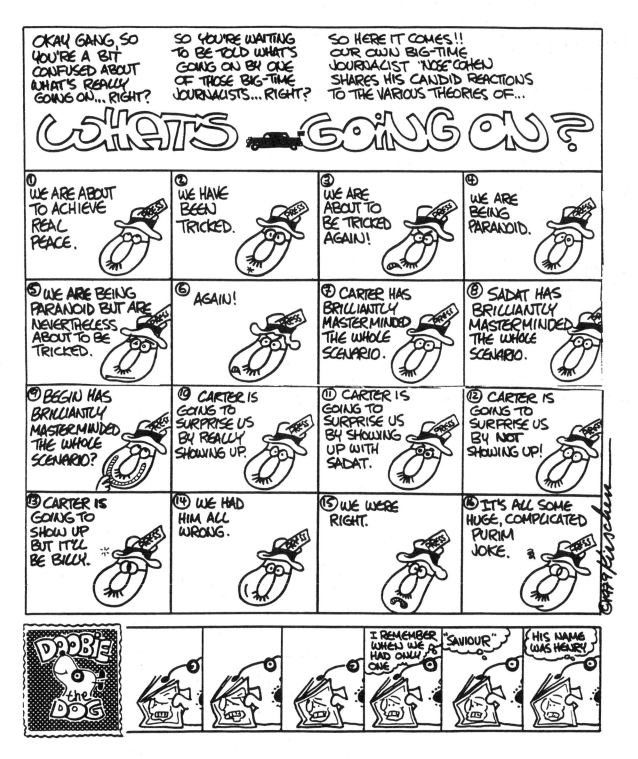

They go ahead and drop a zero from our money and change the name from *lira* to *shekel*. To those of us who are in debt this is maybe not a bad thing?

The Weekend Dry Bones

Worried? Look at the sunny side!

The Weekend Dry Bones

A DAY AT THE BEACH

Dry Bones

The Weekend Dry Bones

REMEMBER WHEN YOU WERE A KID AND YOU WENT TO THE MOVIES? ...

AND THERE WERE THE **GOOD** GUYS

AND THERE WERE THE **BAD** GUYS

AND YOU USED TO WONDER IF THE BAD GUYS **KNEW** THAT THEY WERE THE BAD GUYS?

WELL GANG, FACE IT! WE'VE BEEN CONDEMNED BY **EVERYBODY** SO WE **MUST** BE THE BAD GUYS! AND IF WE WANT TO BE GOOD...

WE'VE GOT TO LEARN TO ACT LIKE THE GOOD GUYS DO

FOR EXAMPLE WE COULD...

SELL ATOMIC BOMBS TO A RABID UNSTABLE REGIME...

LIKE THE FRENCH DID.

SLAUGHTER WHALES AND PORPOISES...

LIKE THE JAPANESE DO.

BREAK OFF DIPLOMATIC RELATIONS WITH A FRIENDLY COUNTRY FOR A PRICE...

SALE

LIKE THE AFRICANS DID.

STICK ALL OUR "NATIVES" IN CAMPS...

RESERVATION

LIKE THE AMERICANS DID.

APOLOGISE FOR FREEDOM OF EXPRESSION ON OUR TELEVISION...

DEATH OF A MORALITY

LIKE THE BRITISH DID.

BEAT BLIND DEMONSTRATORS AND FORCE STERILIZATION...

LIKE THE INDIANS DID.

DRIVE OUR REFUGEES INTO THE SEA IN RICKETY BOATS...

LIKE THE ASIANS DO.

BAR ALL "NON-BELIEVERS" FROM ENTERING OUR HOLY CITY...

STAY OUT

LIKE THE SAUDIS DO

AND OF COURSE WE'D SELL OUT ANYBODY FOR OIL...

WHERE'D EVERYBODY GO?

LIKE EVERYBODY DOES!

Dry Bones

The Weekend Dry Bones

THE ELECTION HAS POINTED UP THE NEED FOR **BASIC** CHANGES IN THE SYSTEM! A PROBLEM TOO COMPLICATED FOR THE DRYBONES STAFF, YOU SAY? **HAH!**... WE PROUDLY PRESENT...

THE DRYBONES PLANS FOR ELECTORAL REFORM

GRUNT! BIFF! BAM! SOCKO! POW! OOF!

PLAN 1

MOST VOTERS CAST BALLOTS FOR THE BIG PARTIES BECAUSE THEY HAD ONLY ONE VOTE AND DIDN'T WANT TO "WASTE IT"

SOME FOOLS FIGURE THAT THIS MEANS WE NEED A TWO-PARTY SYSTEM. **NONSENSE!** WE **DON'T** NEED A TWO **PARTY** SYSTEM!

WE NEED A TWO-**VOTE** SYSTEM!

ONE VOTE FOR A BIG PARTY AND **ONE** FOR A PARTY YOU WANT TO VOTE FOR!

PLAN 2

MOST VOTERS CAST THEIR VOTES **AGAINST** SOMEBODY

WE NEED A NEGATIVE VOTE SYSTEM IN WHICH EVERY PARTY STARTS OUT WITH 120 KNESSET SEATS AND THEN...

EVERYBODY VOTES **AGAINST** THE PARTY OF THEIR CHOOSING

TAKE THAT YOU DIRTY DOG!

A PARTY THAT GETS 15% OF THE "NO-VOTE" LOSES 15% OF ITS SEATS, ETC.

AARGH!

PLAN 3

MOST VOTERS WANTED TO VOTE FOR SOME SMALL PARTY BUT ANTI-DEMOCRATIC BIG PARTIES TOLD THEM THEY SHOULDN'T.

BIG PARTIES, PLAYING THE BIG NUMBERS GAME SELL-OUT, MOVE TOWARDS BLURRING POLITICAL DIFFERENCES AND LUST AFTER POWER

THE OBVIOUS SOLUTION? **BAN BIG PARTIES!** ANY PARTY WITH MORE THAN EIGHT SEATS WILL BE BROKEN UP!...

LIKE THE GREEDY MONOPOLIES THAT THEY ARE.

AAARGH!

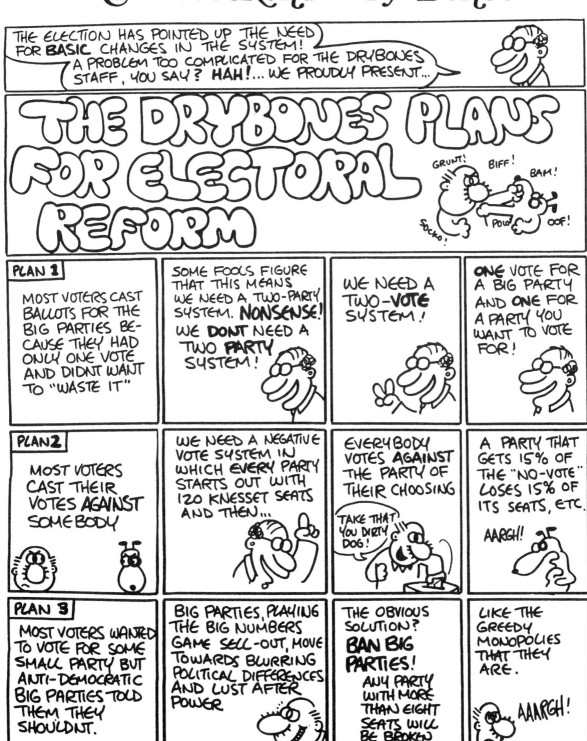

Islamic fundamentalists assassinate Sadat.

The Weekend Dry Bones

The Weekend Dry Bones

ME AND MY UNCLE SAM

Rockets plow into our northern cities. Civilians are forced to sleep in underground bomb shelters. We respond to the continuing military attacks from Lebanon, and the question is . . .

Dry Bones

Dry Bones

WE SHOULD FIX THE PLO UP WITH....

SNAPPY BLUE UNIFORMS AND SEND THEM OFF TO BE....

THE PERMANENT UN INT'L PEACE-KEEPING FORCE!

AND THEN THE NEXT TIME TWO COUNTRIES HAVE A DISPUTE....

THE UN COULD THREATEN TO SEND THEM THE PLO!

JUST THE THREAT WOULD BE ENOUGH!

©1982

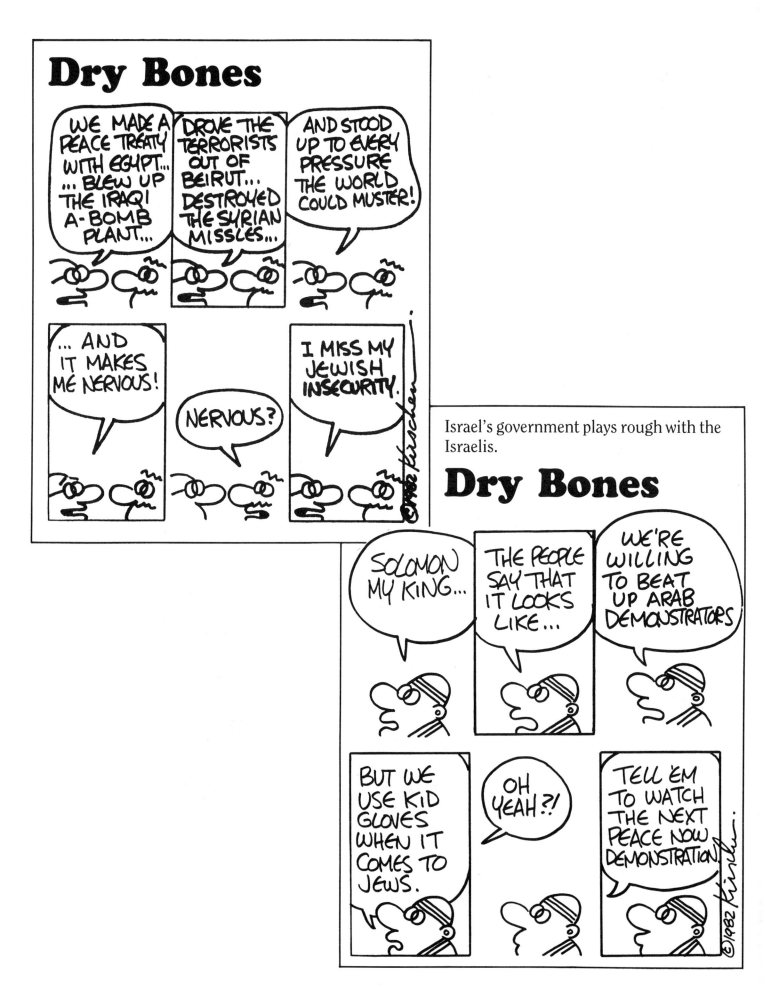

Israel's government plays rough with the Israelis.

The economy is expanding and Israelis start playing the stock market . . . and, like when we start playing on the highway . . . there are crashes.

The Friday Dry Bones

A visit from President Carter.

Dry Bones

The Friday Dry Bones

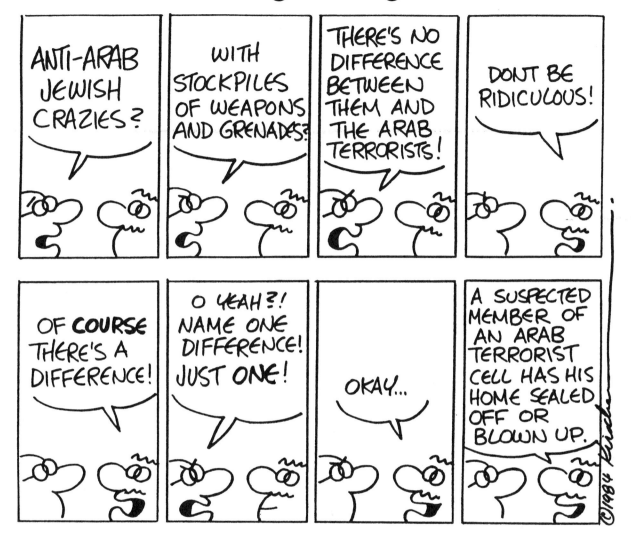

Dry Bones

OFF THE TRACK?

The "peace" with Egypt is stalled, Sadat is dead, and the IDF seems to be stuck inside Lebanon . . . and it feels like somehow, somewhere, we've gotten off the track. We are split politically and are deeply divided over the issue of the war in Lebanon and the settlement of the West Bank. We are living with runaway inflation and, when we all march down to the polls to decide on the future, the results are a dead heat! The electorate is split exactly down the middle. Instead of an answer, we've got another question: "How can you form a coalition government when the two main parties end up in a tie?" We will soon find out.

Dry Bones

Dry Bones

The Friday Dry Bones

Dry Bones

The Friday Dry Bones

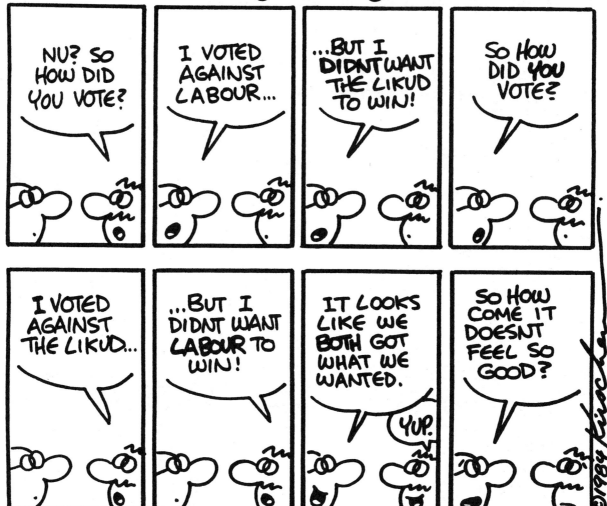

The Friday Dry Bones

So we had elections. So there was a dead heat tie between Labor and the Likud. So the party leaders decide on a unique solution . . . power sharing in a "unity government." But who would be the actual Prime Minister? Hey, let's have two part-time heads of State. They could take turns . . . first one, and then the other. Rotation . . . or as we learned to say in Israeli Hebrew . . . *rotatzia*.

Dry Bones

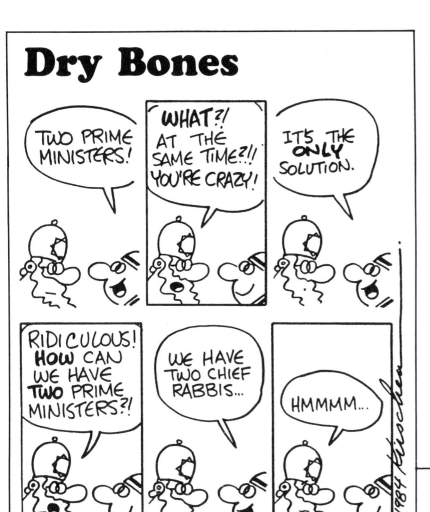

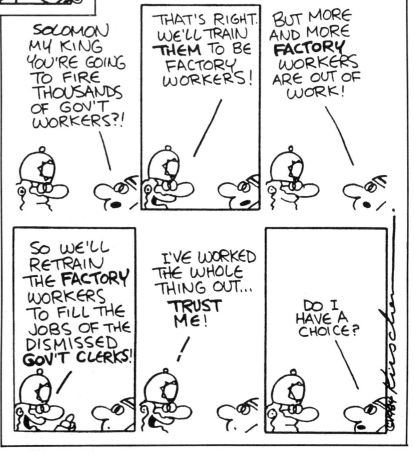

Like the two chief rabbis. . . but more so.

The two big parties *could* have set up a unity coalition government by themselves. . . and thus be free at last from the bullying of the little parties. . . . On the *other* hand. . .

Dry Bones

THE PROBLEM WITH A NARROW-BASED GOV'T...

IS THAT IT IS AT THE MERCY OF THE LITTLE PARTIES.

SO WE HAVE A BROAD-BASED GOV'T OF NATIONAL UNITY.

WHICH IS AT THE MERCY OF THE LITTLE PARTIES!?

SOLOMON MY KING...

YOU ARE STARTING TO UNDERSTAND THE SYSTEM.

The Friday Dry Bones

Dry Bones

We begin pulling out of Lebanon. Our boys are coming home . . . again! And uh . . . the withdrawal is violating the Sabbath?? (*Shabbes* in the Yiddish spoken by the ḥaredi community.)

Dry Bones

113

Dry Bones

MUNCH CRUNCH

CHOMP CRACK CRUNCH

AS SEASONAL A SOUND AS THE RUSTLE OF AUTUMN LEAVES...

OR THE CRUNCH OF WINTER SNOW UNDER FOOT..

IT'S THE MATZAH MUNCHING OF SPRING.

CRUNCH CRACKLE CRUNCH

©1985

The Friday Dry Bones

The government hates it when the public is smarter than **it** is.

The Friday Dry Bones

... AND A HAPPY NEW YEAR TO US ALL

Dry Bones

YOU GO TO SLEEP NOT KNOWING...

IF THERE'S A STRIKE OR SCHOOL IN THE MORNING!

IT MAKES ME ANGRY

IT MAKES ME NERVOUS

AND IT DRIVES ME CRAZY!!

IT'S PRO'BLY GOOD TRAINING FOR BEING A GROWN-UP.

The Friday Dry Bones

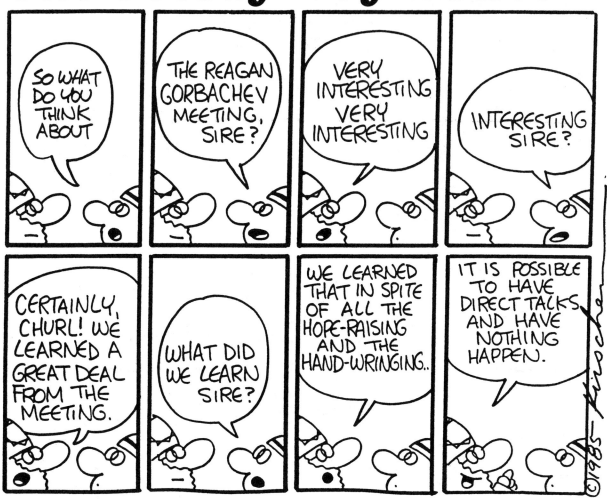

Dry Bones

ANNOUNCING THE DRY BONES DON'T-BE-SURPRISED WHEN-THEY SPRING-THESE ON-YOU

NEW TAX LIST

THUMB TAX

YOU'LL BE ASSESSED FOR EACH OPPOSABLE DIGIT.

TICKS TAX

A CHARGE FOR EACH CLOCK YOU OWN.

POLE TAX

YOU'LL PAY AN EXTRA LEVY IF A POLISH GENTLEMAN LIVES ON YOUR BLOCK.

SAX TAX

(ALSO A FEE FOR VIOLINS, VIOLAS, NOSE-FLUTES, AND PIANOS)

TAX TAX

EVERYTHING ELSE IS TAXED SO WHY NOT TAXES?

© 1986 Kirschen

1986 . . . Everybody gets used to foreign travel . . . even Mr. Shuldig!

Dry Bones

I'M FRESH OFF A PLANE FROM THE STATES.

..MY BELLY IS STILL FULL OF FABULOUS AMERICAN JUNK FOOD.

..AND I HAVEN'T HEARD A SINGLE NEWSCAST YET SO I DON'T KNOW WHAT'S GOING ON.

THE WEATHER HERE IS **BEAUTIFUL** THE COUNTRY LOOKS **GREAT** AND MY MIND IS **BLANK.**

SIGH

IT'S THE ZIONIST DREAM!

© 1986 Kirschen

Dry Bones

THE CHERNOBYL CLOUD HAS RAISED RADIATION LEVELS AROUND THE WORLD.

AHH... BUT THIS ONLY MEANS THAT THE WORLD AVERAGE IS UP...

AND SO "NORMAL" IS NOW HIGHER!... AND WE JUST MOVE A DECIMAL POINT AND EVERYTHING IS OKAY!

THAT IS DEVIOUSLY BRILLIANT, PROFESSOR.

HAVE YOU ALWAYS BEEN IN NUCLEAR SAFEGUARDS?

NO... I USED TO BE IN ISRAELI BANKING.

©1986 Kirschen

Dry Bones

SYRIA IS BACKING THE BEIRUTIS WHO ARE FIGHTING HIZBULLAH.

ISRAEL IS BACKING THE SOUTHERNERS WHO ARE FIGHTING HIZBULLAH.

WHICH PROVES THAT OLD MID-EAST ADAGE...

THE ENEMY OF MINE ENEMY IS MINE ENEMY

..AND DON'T BE TOO SURE ABOUT YOUR "FRIENDS" EITHER

©1988 Kirschen

Dry Bones

Dry Bones

The Friday Dry Bones

YOU KNOW YOU'VE BEEN HERE TOO LONG WHEN...

...YOU PARK ON THE SIDEWALK AND WALK ON THE STREET.

...WHEN YOU JUST CAN'T THINK OF THE WORD IN ENGLISH.

WHEN YOU'RE SHOCKED THAT THE TAXI HAS A METER THAT IS "WORKING" TODAY.

WHEN YOU CAN'T THINK OF ANYTHING THAT THEY DON'T HAVE HERE

PIZZA
CHINESE FOOD
BAGELS
LOX
CREDIT CARDS
SHOPPING MALLS
PAPER PLATES

WHEN YOU STOP BOASTING ABOUT YOUR GOOD RELATIONS WITH YOUR BANK MANAGER

WHEN YOU GET A VIDEO.

WHEN YOU FEEL THAT ROTATING PRIME MINISTERS IS SOMEHOW BETTER THAN MESSY, NOISY EXPENSIVE ELECTIONS

©1986 Kirschen

Dry Bones

The Friday Dry Bones

ONCE UPON A TIME THE GIANT INFLATION STALKED THE LAND

AND HE THREATENED TO DESTROY EVERYTHING!

BUT ONE DAY THE PEOPLE SAID "ENOUGH"!

ENOUGH

AND THE SPIRIT OF THE NEW ISRAEL WAS BORN

SPIRIT NI

AND AFTER WHAT SEEMED LIKE A RATHER SHORT BATTLE, THE GIANT FELL!

PLOTZ

AND SOME SAID THAT HE WAS DEAD AND SOME SAID THAT HE WAS ONLY KNOCKED OUT BY A FALLING DOLLAR.

AND THERE WAS A PUZZLEMENT IN THE LAND...

WHAT TH'?

FOR NOBODY KNEW WHAT EXACTLY HAD GONE RIGHT.

SPIRIT NI

©1986

The Friday Dry Bones

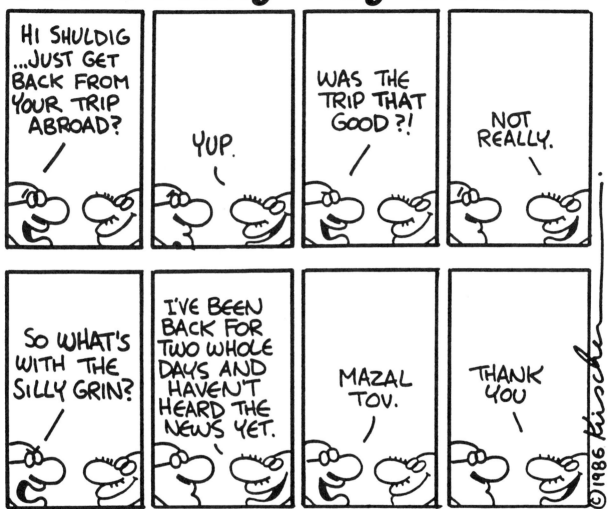

The government is talking about finally dumping our phony socialist system in favor of a phony capitalist system.

The Friday Dry Bones

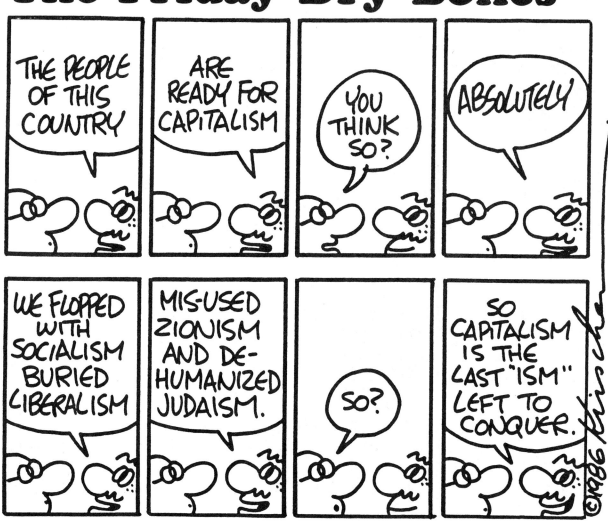

The Friday Dry Bones

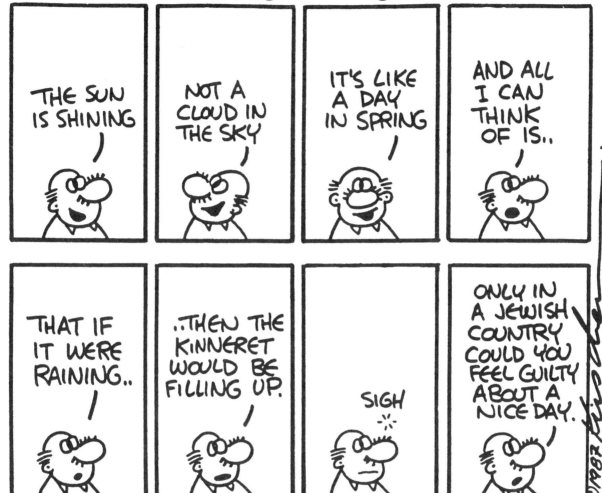

It's January. The rainy season is supposed to be at its very strongest. Israel's agriculture depends on the winter downpour. *Where* are the rains?!!

Dry Bones

Dry Bones

April 1987 . . . Kirschen is off to the States on a speaking tour. . . . Mr. Shuldig and his dog Doobie apprise the public of *their* trip.

The Friday Dry Bones

Dry Bones

DID I HEAR YOU SAY YOU WERE FROM ISRAEL?

YES, I..

GREAT LITTLE COUNTRY, WE COULD LEARN A LOT FROM YOU PEOPLE..

UH..

YOU'VE GOT UNITY! YOUR SOCIETY ISN'T SPLIT LIKE OURS!

WELL...

IT'S EFFICIENT AND YOU'VE GOT GOOD LEADERSHIP

HMM

OF COURSE YOU PEOPLE HAVE ALWAYS BEEN GOOD AT BUSINESS.

OH

SIP

©1987 Kirschen

The *shuk* is the Middle Eastern bazaar or marketplace.

Dry Bones

THIS IS AN AMERICAN SHOPPING MALL...

HUNDREDS OF SPECIALTY STORES AND STALLS...

AND THE SHOPPERS JUST STROLL ALONG...

SHOPPING, OR LOOKING, OR HAVING SOME FAST FOODS...

IT'S AN AMAZING AMERICAN MARKETING CONCEPT!

IT'S A SHUK.

©1987 Kirschen

Dry Bones

The Friday Dry Bones

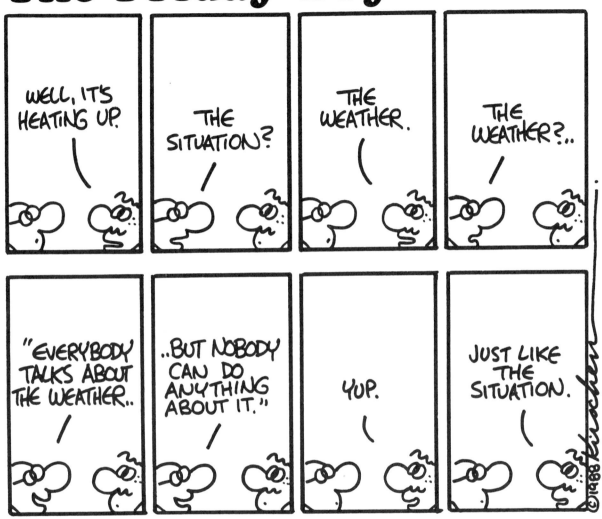

Dry Bones

Rioting Arab mobs begin stone-throwing attacks. We *must* stop their assaults, but we *can't* just gun them down . . . unless, maybe . . . if we used rubber bullets?

The Friday Dry Bones

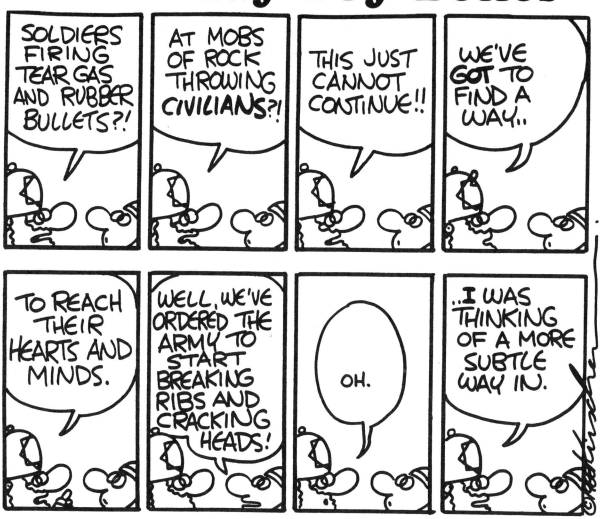

Media clout!

Dry Bones

IF AFTER TWENTY YEARS OF OUR OCCUPATION

...THEY HATE US **SO** MUCH

DOES THAT TELL US SOMETHING ABOUT **US**?

OR ABOUT **THEM**?

OR ABOUT TWENTY YEARS?

OR ABOUT OCCUPATION?

©1988 Kirschen

Dry Bones

George Shultz is pressuring the Arabs with a new American plan.

Dry Bones

 THEY REJECTED A STATE IN 1948..

 AUTONOMY IN 1979

AND SHULTZ IN 1988

 YOU'VE **GOT** TO FEEL SORRY FOR THE PALESTINIANS.

 ...THEY'VE GOT LEADERSHIP THAT'S..

EVEN DUMBER THAN OURS!

CBS catches the IDF beating up prisoners.

Dry Bones

OKAY...

 SO WE DIDN'T BELIEVE IT WHEN **THEY** SAID IT

 AND WE WOULDN'T BELIEVE IT WHEN **RABIN** SAID IT

 BUT IF WE WON'T BELIEVE IT

 AFTER CBS NEWS FILMED IT...

 ...THEN WHAT HAVE WE BECOME?

An anti-Israeli terrorist leader is killed in his home by a mysterious hit team.

The Friday Dry Bones

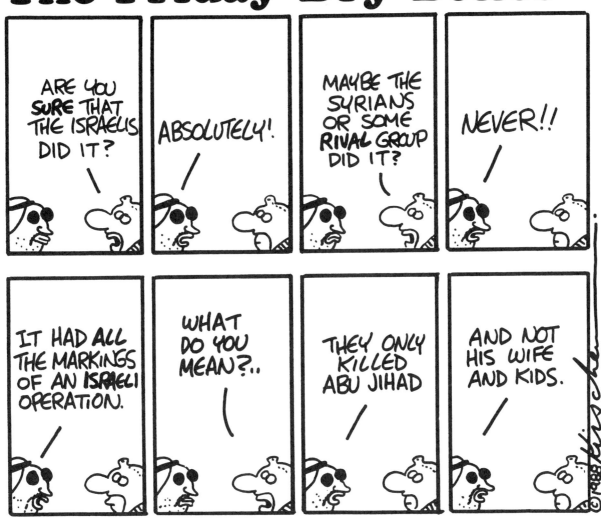

Dry Bones

ABC TV
IS DOING
A SHOW
CALLED

"NIGHTLINE
FROM THE
HOLY LAND"

...THEY
WOULD HAVE
CALLED IT..

"NIGHTLINE
FROM
ISRAEL"

BUT THEY'RE
BEING TOO
EVEN-HANDED
TO RECOGNIZE

..THE
EXISTENCE
OF OUR
STATE.

©1988 Kirschen

The Friday Dry Bones

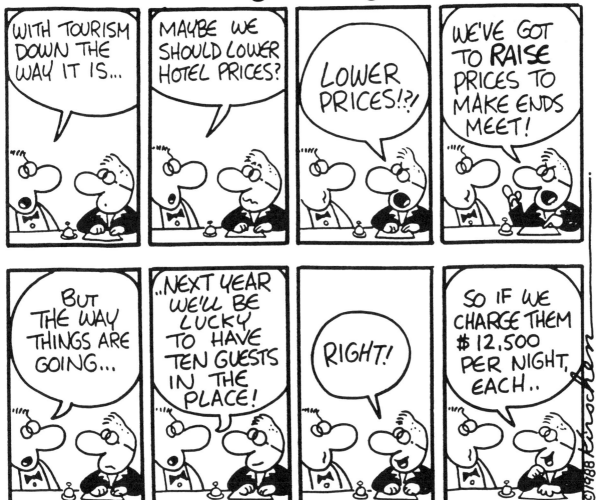

Dry Bones

THE CURIOUS THING IS THAT..

BY THEIR READINESS TO BURN UP THE LAND,

THEY SHOW US ALL

THAT DEEP IN **THEIR** HEARTS

IT IS **THEIR** BELIEF,

THAT THIS LAND IS OURS,

©1988 Kirschen

Dry Bones

WHEN WILL THEY LET US HAVE A SECOND TV STATION?

I FIGURE IT'S NECK AND NECK WITH THE

CAPTURE OF THE LOCH NESS MONSTER

... AND SAN FRANCISCO SLIDING INTO THE SEA.

ANYONE OF THEM **COULD** HAPPEN TOMORROW

OR IT COULD BE A MUCH LONGER WAIT.

©1988 Kirschen

Dry Bones

Dry Bones

NEW OPENINGS

The gates of the Soviet Union are about to swing wide open and the entire Iron Curtain is about to collapse. The captive Jews of Russia, the former Soviet republics, and Eastern Europe will be free to come home to us! Our government is secretly arranging to ransom the black Jews of Ethiopia and bring them home to this, their ancient homeland. Secret talks will soon lead to the Madrid Peace Conference. We don't know it yet, but the future is about to get brighter than we could imagine. Another thing that we don't know about yet is that the world will soon ask us to become sitting ducks for Saddam Hussein's Scud missiles.

Dry Bones

Dry Bones

AZERIS
FIGHTING
ARMENIANS

SLAVS
FIGHTING
ALBANIANS

PAKISTANIS
AGAINST
INDIANS

IT'S SORT OF
NICE THAT
THESE DAYS..

..ISRAEL
ISN'T THE
ONLY...

"BAD BOY"
IN THE
SCHOOL YARD!

Another birthday.

Dry Bones

HAD HER FRIENDS DESERTED HER BECAUSE OF HER LIMITATIONS OR THEIRS??

OR MAYBE BOTH??

IN ANY CASE, HER LOST SONS WERE COMING FROM RUSSIA AND ETHIOPIA

AND IF THIS IMPOSSIBLE DREAM COULD COME TRUE..

SHE WOULD CONTINUE TO DREAM OF PEACE...

SHE WAS FORTY TWO AND SHE WAS STILL VERY YOUNG.

©1990 Kirschen

Once again local idealists are calling for election reform. Not one of the many *Dry Bones* proposals is even being mentioned!!

Dry Bones

ISRAELIS ARE NOW DEMANDING

A RADICAL CHANGE IN GOVERNMENT

REALLY?

YUP

WHAT'S IT CALLED?

MAJORITY RULE.

©1990 Kirschen

153

Dry Bones

Dry Bones

It's the Jewish New Year and we answer a calendar question.

Dry Bones

SOLOMON MY KING

WHY IS IT THAT FOR THE REST OF THE WORLD

THE YEAR IS 1990...

BUT FOR US IT'S ALREADY NEW YEAR 5751?!

IT'S BECAUSE MORE HAPPENS TO US!

YES, IT'S OUR ANNUAL SHANA TOVA DRY BONES.

Dry Bones

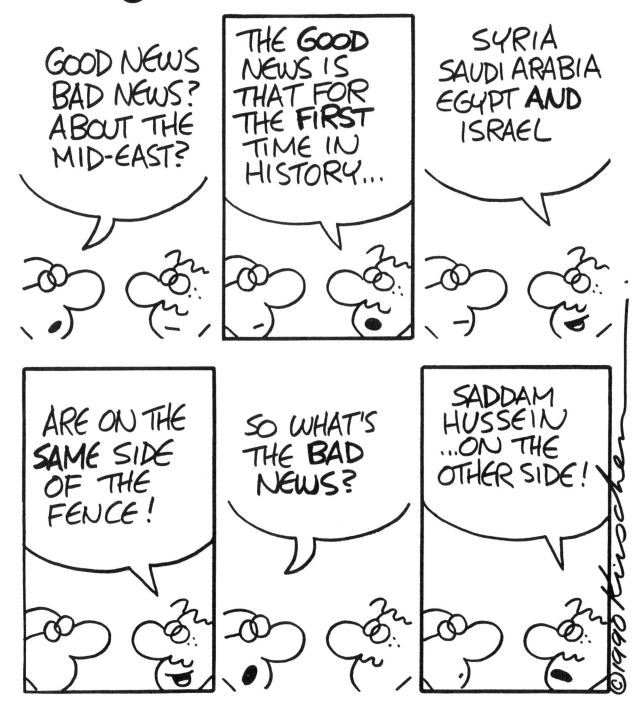

Dry Bones

ROSH HASHANA THE JEWISH NEW YEAR

A TIME OF EXAMINING GOOD AND EVIL

A TIME OF PRAYER AND CONTEMPLATION

AND **THIS YEAR** AS THE NATIONS GATHER TO STOP SADDAM

AS WE PRAY FOR A HAPPIER AND SAFER WORLD...

THE WHOLE CIVILIZED WORLD IS PRAYING WITH US.

© 1990 Kirschen

Dry Bones

EXCUSE ME SIR... YOU WORK HERE AS A LUGGAGE HANDLER...

AT ISRAEL'S BEN GURION INTERNATIONAL AIRPORT...

WHERE THOUSANDS OF RUSSIAN JEWS ARRIVE EACH DAY!

COULD YOU TELL OUR VIEWERS WHAT THE NEWCOMERS ARE LIKE?

WELL... THE FEW WHO AREN'T CARRYING VIOLIN CASES

..ARE THE PIANISTS.

© 1990 Kirschen

Dry Bones

Dry Bones

The Scud war . . . how will future generations of Israelis remember these terrible days as we sit in sealed rooms waiting to be hit by the next round of Iraqi missiles?

Operation Shlomo and the rescue of the Soviet Jews . . . as it felt on the ground in Israel.

Dry Bones
©1991 *Kirschen*

THE MORNING AFTER

WELL... WE MIDDLE-EASTERNERS FINALLY DID IT!

KLIK!

FACE TO FACE IN MADRID.

...AND WITH THE WHOLE WORLD WATCHING.

OKAY! ...SO **NOBODY** KNOWS WHAT THE FUTURE WILL BE.

BUT ONE THING IS **SURE!**

THINGS WILL **NEVER** BE THE SAME AGAIN!

KLIK!

DOOBIE the DOG

OF COURSE THERE **ARE** HISTORIC MILESTONES THAT CHANGE ABSOLUTELY **NOTHING**...

BUT THAT KEEP ON HAPPENING ANYWAY.

...LIKE AGREEMENTS IN **LEBANON** OR CEASE-FIRES IN **YUGOSLAVIA!**

Dry Bones

©1991 Kirschen.

WE CAN IMPROVE ROAD SAFETY!

IF WE'D ADOPT A FEW SIMPLE PROPOSALS...

CHANGE ALL THE "WALK-DON'T WALK" SIGNALS TO "DON'T WALK DON'T WALK" SIGNALS

ELIMINATE ALL ZEBRA CROSSINGS

...THEY ONLY LURE PEDESTRIANS INTO THE FLOW OF TRAFFIC.

HONK!

SPLAT

IF THEY WANT TO WALK LET 'EM GO TO A PEDESTRIAN MALL...WHERE THEY BELONG!

MAKE MORE SIGNS FOR REAR WINDOWS

BEGINNERS

NEW DRIVER

1012

ALL OTHERS

DANGEROUS DRIVER

2031

USE PEDESTRIAN DECOYS

..A SIMPLE WAY TO REDUCE YOUR CHANCES OF BEING HIT BY 50%!

AND BECAUSE SO MANY ACCIDENTS ARE CAUSED BY ISRAELI DRIVERS "LOSING CONTROL" OF THEIR VEHICLES

CARS THAT HAVE BEEN INVOLVED IN ACCIDENTS SHOULD BE SHOT!

BANG

DOOBIE the DOG

Q. WHY DID THE CHICKEN REFUSE TO CROSS THE ROAD?

A. BECAUSE HE WASN'T A FRYER!

Dry Bones

JEWISH NEW YEAR VERSUS NEW YEAR'S EVE!

"Don't worry" was the message of this Scud war *Dry Bones* for our overseas friends.

Dry Bones

Dry Bones

Operation Shlomo was what we called the massive airlift that brought our Ethiopian brothers and sisters home to Israel.

Dry Bones

Dry Bones

Don't raise the bridge . . . lower the water.

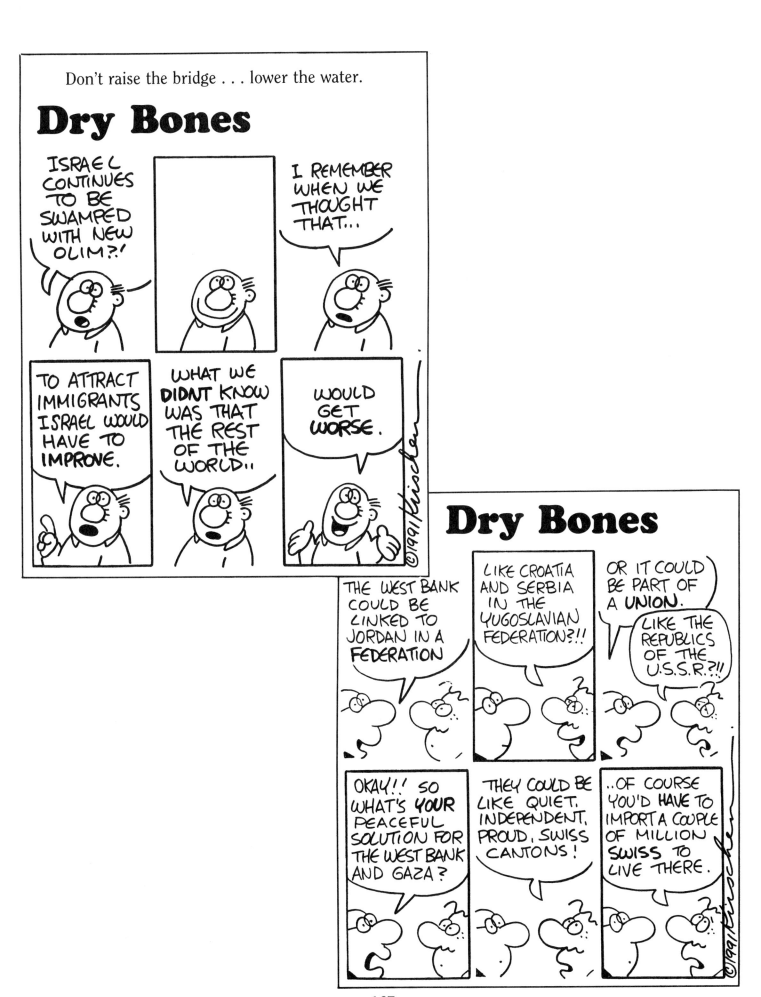

A quick look at the flood of new immigrants living among us . . . before we get on with the business of ignoring them.

Bureaucratic problems.

Dry Bones

THE "COMMITTEE TO SAVE SOVIET JEWRY" HAS CHANGED ITS NAME?

YES.

IT'S NOW THE "COMMITTEE TO SAVE JEWS FROM RUSSIA, UKRANIA, UZBEKISTAN,...

...BELORUSSIA, LATVIA, MOLDOVA, TAJIKISTAN, AZERBAIJAN,...

...ARMENIA, LITHUANIA, GEORGIA, ESTONIA, **AND** KYRGYZSTAN."

Dry Bones

172

Dry Bones

If they were *really* interested in reforesting the planet they would have invited the Jewish National Fund to the Save the Earth conference in Rio.

Dry Bones

Another difference between Israel and America.

Dry Bones

Dry Bones

Dry Bones

Dry Bones

IN THE 21ST CENTURY, LITTLE ISRAEL WILL BE ONE OF THE **LARGEST** COUNTRIES IN THE WORLD!!...

KRAKPOTIA   EAST KRAKPOTIA   REP TAD

...NOT BECAUSE **WE'LL** BE GETTING ANY BIGGER...

NORTH MOSCOW   EAST MONACO   SLO

BUT BECAUSE THE **REST** OF THE WORLD IS BREAKING...

NORTH-WEST MACEDONIA   VENICE BEACHIA   MOLDAVIA

...INTO **SMALLER** AND **SMALLER** PIECES!!

UPPER WALES   ISRAEL   BUNGI JUMPIA   SOUTH GEORGIA

DOOBIE the DOG

THEY USED TO SAY THAT ISRAEL WAS "TOO SMALL A STATE TO SURVIVE!" WELL, WE'VE BEEN **SUCH** A SUCCESS THAT...

NOW EVERY **OTHER** TWO-BIT MINORITY WANTS A MINI-STATE OF ITS OWN!

Hamas fundamentalists start calling for the murder of Jews. We deport four hundred of them to Lebanon. The outside world is *not* amused!

Dry Bones

Another birthday.

Dry Bones

Dry Bones

Cable TV comes to Israel and we get to see what the rest of the world gets to see.

Dry Bones

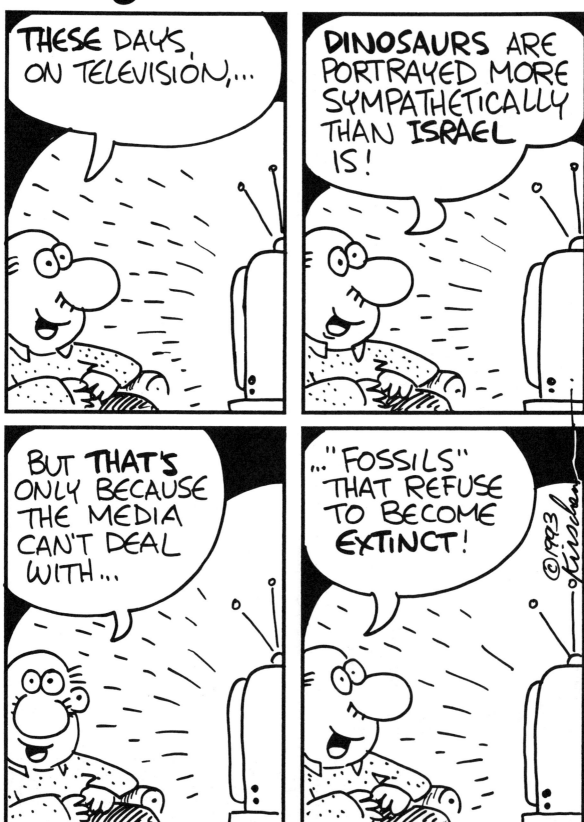

THE BUMPY ROAD

The country is about to be hit by a new wave of Terrorist Suicide bombings, Katyusha missile attacks from Lebanon, and by the assassination of our Prime Minister. Rough times. But this the chapter, which ends our book is, of course, the opening chapter of the future that awaits us. We know that in the end we will fulfill our mission to become a light unto the nations, that in the end, humanity has no choice other than to heed the words of our ancient prophets and to beat its swords into plowshares and to study war no more. In the meantime, we will continue to plant our trees and to reclaim the barren desert lands. We will continue, through our scientific and technological research and development, to seek the answers to the problems that face our planet. And we will continue to show our love for each other with cynicism and sarcasm. We are on the bumpy road to peace.

Dry Bones

Dry Bones

BY BLOWING UP EGYPTIANS AND ISRAELIS AND TRYING TO KILL JORDAN'S KING HUSSEIN

THE ISLAMIC FANATICS ARE PROVIDING THE STATES OF THE REGION

...WITH THE ONE MISSING INGREDIENT FOR REAL PEACE! ?

...A COMMON ENEMY.

Sukkot . . . the biblical Feast of Tabernacles.

Dry Bones

SHULDIG AND HIS DOG, DOOBIE

SUKKOT! THE HOLIDAY IN WHICH WE ARE SUPPOSED TO SIT IN FLIMSY "BOOTHS"...

PERHAPS AS A REMINDER OF THE FRAILTY OF OUR EXISTENCE!

WE NEED A REMINDER?

The leopard changes his spots?

Dry Bones

AFTER **YEARS** OF BLOOD-THIRSTY TERRORISM AND GANG LEADERSHIP

CURRENT DEVELOPMENTS DEMAND THAT I CHANGE MY APPROACH, MY STYLE...

BUT CHAIRMAN ARAFAT...

UH... CALL ME PRESIDENT.

©1993 Kirschen

Dry Bones

AFTER **45 YEARS** OF TERRORISM, **HOLY WARS,** INTERNATIONAL ISOLATION, **INFLATION,** RECESSION...

NO IMMIGRATION, **MASSIVE** IMMIGRATION, **SCUD MISSILE ATTACKS** AND ECONOMIC BOYCOTT...

...PEACE WITH OUR NEIGHBORS?

WOW!

JUST WHEN WE THOUGHT THAT THERE WERE NO NEW CHALLENGES **LEFT** FOR ISRAEL TO FACE!

©1993 Kirschen

Dry Bones

PALESTINIAN **TERRORIST** ATTACKS AGAINST ISRAELI JEWS?!!

TRUE...

...BUT THOSE ARE **HAMAS** PALESTINIANS!

INTERESTING!

...AS **SOON** AS ISRAEL RECOGNIZED THE **PLO**...THE REST OF THE WORLD **SUDDENLY** DISCOVERED THAT

THE PLO IS **NO LONGER** THE SOLE LEGITIMATE REPRESENTATIVE OF THE PALESTINIAN PEOPLE!

Examining the lessons of history.

Dry Bones

GREAT EMPIRES **SINK** INTO **CHAOS**! FROM BABYLON TO THE **SOVIETS** WE JEWS HAVE **SEEN IT ALL**!!

AND THE JEWISH PEOPLE **NEVER** FORGETS! ...WE **NEVER** FORGET!

WOW!

AND DO YOU KNOW **WHY** WE NEVER FORGET?

NO... WHY?

IT'S BECAUSE WE HAVE A **MEMORY DISORDER**.

Dry Bones

Dry Bones

It's a revolution in communications! We've jumped from *one* channel of government-run television to forty-four channels of cable TV! But will this change us? Will heroic Samsons turn into Homer Simpsons?!!

Dry Bones

Dry Bones

Dry Bones

The terrorist war against us continues to escalate. The PLO chief seems content.

Dry Bones

A slaughter of Moslems at prayer in Hebron. We are horrified.

Dry Bones

Dry Bones

Dry Bones

Dry Bones

VIRTUAL REALITY GAMES HAVE COME TO ISRAEL!

"VIRTUAL REALITY"??

THAT'S WHERE YOU "EXIST" IN A **TV FANTASY SO REAL** AND SO **CLOSE** THAT YOU CAN **ALMOST** BELIEVE THAT IT **IS** REAL!

WOW!... LIKE THE PALESTINIAN PEACE PROCESS?!

©1994 Kirschen

Dry Bones

THE **FIRST** STEP TO PEACE WAS WHEN ISRAELI TROOPS...

...STOPPED ACTING LIKE POLICEMEN IN GAZA!

THE **SECOND** STEP TO PEACE WILL BE WHEN THE PALESTINIAN "POLICE"...

...**START** ACTING LIKE POLICEMEN IN GAZA!

©1994 Kirschen

The king of Jordan reaches out a hand of friendship . . . and talks to the Israeli public with understanding and respect.

Dry Bones

Dry Bones

Another year rolls by . . . and more and more we seem to be living in the future . . . which, in some ways, is not quite as real as the past.

Dry Bones

Dry Bones

We gather round our TV sets to witness the formerly unthinkable.

Dry Bones

And so the years roll by.

Dry Bones

Tu B'Shvat, the Jewish New Year of the Trees.

Dry Bones

Dry Bones

Yitzhak Rabin, Prime Minister of Israel, is assassinated.

Dry Bones

Dry Bones

THE RABIN ASSASSINATION SHOULD TEACH US THAT...

WHEN WE USE THE WORD "THEY"...

AND WE'RE TALKING ABOUT US...

THEN WE'RE RIPPING OURSELVES APART.

© 1995 Kirschen

Dry Bones

ISRAEL IS BEING FORCED TO NEGOTIATE WITH...

...THE TERRORIST STATE OF SYRIA.

YUP.

IT'S JUST AWFUL.

I KNOW.

I WISH WE HAD NICER ENEMIES.

© 1995 Kirschen

Dry Bones

The elections of 1996.

Dry Bones

Dry Bones

Dry Bones

There seems to be only one way to complete our journey through the history of the Jewish state . . . with this holiday cartoon of hope for the future.

Dry Bones

GLOSSARY

aliya In Hebrew, literally "going up." The act of a Jew when he or she immigrates to live in Israel. It also applies to the act of a community of Jews, as in the massive "Russian" aliya or the miraculous "Ethiopian" aliya. The great wave of aliya from America has not yet taken place.

Ashkenazi The old Hebrew for "German." A Jew whose family originally came from Europe and whose roots are therefore in western culture.

bakbook Bottle. The word attempts to imitate the sound of fluid being poured from a bottle.

brit mila Jewish ritual circumcision.

botz Mud. Slang for our dark, thick "turkish" coffee.

Diaspora The "exile" in fancy English. In Hebrew the word in Galut. It refers to the lands in which the Jewish people were forced to live after being uprooted from our ancient homeland. Jews who live in America, England, France, Argentina, Syria, or any place that is not Israel, are living in the Diaspora.

fryer A chump.

fooya Hebrew slang word used by children to express distaste and disapproval.

> "What do you think of your new homeroom teacher?"
>
> "FOOYA!"

gan Kindergarten or garden.

> "Today was your first day in gan. Did you like it?"
>
> "Fooya!"

gever A man. Often used to describe a "real man."

> "Okay, so you don't like your new kindergarten teacher, but that's no reason to cry. Be a gever!"

Hamas An Islamic terrorist organization based in Gaza and the West Bank.

haredi Ultra Orthodox.

heder In Hebrew, literally a room. When pronounced with a Yiddish accent it refers to the old-style, European, one room, religious Hebrew schools.

heshbon Arithmetic, also used for the bill, as in "The meal in this restaurant was wonderful, but wait 'til we see the heshbon!"

Hizbullah An Islamic terrorist organization based in Lebanon.

hutz la'aretz Outside of Israel.

> "I've just returned from a trip to hutz la'aretz."
>
> "Big deal. I was born there."

IDF Israel Defense Forces (the Israeli military).

Intifada Arabic for "shaking." The Intifada was (is?) a violent Palestinian insurrection to "shake off" Israeli government rule.

JNF The Jewish National Fund. Originally set up to collect funds for the purchase of land in "Palestine" for the Jewish homeland, it later became the vehicle for restoring the land by the planting of trees. Today the JNF is mostly involved in building water reservoirs and planting forests in Israel.

Kach activist Kach was the political movement set up in Israel by Rabbi Meir Kahane. The organization was declared illegal, but there are still a number of "Kach activists" around.

Kinneret The Sea of Galilee.

Knesset Israel's parliament.

Kupat Holim The sick fund, Israel's take-a-seat-and-wait-your-turn version of socialized medicine.

k'viut Tenure.

Labor The socialist party of Ben Gurion, Golda Meir, Yitzhak Rabin, and Shimon Peres.

Lavon affair Cover-up of a botched Israeli secret operation in Egypt during the Ben Gurion years.

Likud The right-wing party of Menachem Begin and Binyamin Netanyahu.

lira The name of the Israeli currency we used from 1948 until we went back to the biblically proper term shekel.

Lubovitch Rebbe Charismatic leader of Ha-bad, one of the largest hasidic sects.

makolet Grocery store.

mazal tov Good luck.

Mitzpe Ramon Israeli development town in the Negev, predominantly Sephardi.

mossaka Eggplant delicacy.

Nahmunshai After Nachman Shai, the army spokesman who lulled us into believing that we were safe while Saddam Hussein shot Scud missiles at us.

NRP The National Religious Party.

olim Olim are the Jews who come to Israel on aliya. It is commonly accepted that here in Israel we love aliya but not the olim.

Pollard affair Israel's version of the "If you should get caught we will, of course, deny any responsibility in the matter."

puncture Israeli slang for a flat tire, and, by extension, slang for any unexpected foul-up.

pushka Tin charity box.

rotatzia Slang for the only-in-Israel idea of rotating prime ministers after an election tie. The only time we ever had rotatzia was when Likud's Shamir and Labor's Peres agreed to share a term. It didn't work out to be any worse (or better) than having one PM per term.

Sabra The prickly-on-the-outside but-sweet-and-mushy-on-the-inside cactus fruit. Israeli slang for native-born Israelis who, in theory, are sweet and mushy on the inside but . . . oh well, you get it.

Sephardi Literally "a Spaniard." Used to define an "oriental" Jew (from the Middle Eastern countries) whose roots go back to Spain. Almost all Jews are either Ashkenazi or Sephardi. Others, like the Jews of Ethiopia don't fit into either category and are thus considered to be exotics.

Shabbes Yiddish for the Hebrew word Shabbat. Shabbat means Sabbath, religious demonstrators denouncing violations of the Sabbath shout Shabbes rather than Shabbat.

shana tova Happy New Year.

shekel The name of the Israeli currency we used in ancient times, and today in the born-again State of Israel.

sherut　Hebrew for service. A taxicab that carries a group of passengers and has a per seat fare is called a sherut.

shlichim　Emissaries. Aliya shlichim are the guys who tried to get Jews to come home to the Jewish state. Every immigrant from the West has a shaliach lurking in his or her background. Ethiopian Jews and Sephardi Jews we just loaded onto planes and boats.

Shouf　An area of Lebanon.

shuk　An open air market.

shuldig　The Yiddish word for guilt. Shuldig, with a capital S is the name of the bald guy in the Dry Bones cartoons.

smokh　To rely upon. To trust. "Smokh alai" means "Trust me." When an Israeli merchant or tradesman says it, don't.

Sussita　The neat little Israeli automobile that was going to take over the world of motoring and didn't.

tramp　In Israel when a driver stops to give somebody a lift it's called "a tramp." An Israeli Hitchhiker is thus "a trampiste."

Tu B'Shvat　The 15th of the Hebrew month of Shvat, it is the new year holiday of the trees and the annual tree-planting day of the Jewish people. See JNF.

Vaflim　A nosh that is somewhere between a cookie and a wafer.

Yihyeh tov　"Things will be okay." Something you say to new olim.